Desi Pubs

A guide to
British-Indian Pubs,
Food & Culture

⤜⤜ ⤛⤛

DAVID JESUDASON

CAMRA
BOOKS

Published by the Campaign for Real Ale Ltd
230 Hatfield Road, St Albans, Hertfordshire AL1 4LW
www.camra.org.uk/books

First published 2023
Reprinted 2023

ISBN 978-1-85249-385-1

A CIP catalogue record for this book is available from the British Library

Printed and bound in the UK by Short Run Press Ltd, Exeter.

Managing Editor: Alan Murphy
Design / Typography: Dale Tomlinson
Sales & Marketing: Toby Langdon
Cover: Tida Bradshaw

MIX
Paper from
responsible sources
FSC® C014540

Most of the images used in this book were supplied by the author. The publisher would also like
to thank those establishments who kindly granted permission for their photography to be used.

Contents

(cont.)

Introduction to Desi Pubs

My first intention with this book was to celebrate Asian culture through the lens of British-Indian 'desi' pubs that were set up by the diaspora from the 1960s onwards. I expected them to be places frequented mainly by British-Asians and I had some high-minded – but easily achievable – intentions, such as changing what we expect a publican to be: out with the default of the white middle-aged man and in with Mr Singh.

But what I discovered was there was a certain section of white working-class culture that also needs to be – finally – recognised and celebrated. When I first visited Smethwick in the West Midlands, I was taken aback, not only by how this was an Asian-majority town dealing with a post-industrial world, but how the white population loved their – and 'their' is crucial here – desi pubs.

They lived lives far removed from gentrified areas, with many friends who were Asian, and even knew a smattering of Punjabi. Instead of running away or complaining about 'immigration' these ordinary people embraced change and discovered their lives could be enriched by it. They had more than earned the right to be proud of their desi pubs.

'In a rough and ready way,' says Kieran Connell, history lecturer at Queen's University Belfast, 'they're the vanguard of multiculturalism.'

This book doesn't avoid describing racism and prejudice, but it also looks at the people who embraced their local's new identity and who played a huge role in making them thriving community hubs run by a different sort of landlord.

Desi pubs show what we can achieve when we take on prejudice and fuse the best of two cultures – in this case British and Indian. They also illustrate how we can then successfully – and with little conflict – navigate a post-racism world. This book reflects the stories behind this new beginning, as well as being a guide to the best places to drink pints while eating a sizzling platter. Or, as Harry Mungali in the Black Horse, Hounslow, West London, said: 'You don't want this to be a posh Egon Ronay guide. This has to be David Jesudason's Best Desi Pubs.' Let's hope I've not let Harry down.

And if you're not sure about stepping into an unfamiliar world with groups who have a different cultural background to you, then I have your back. Being of Indian and Malay origin means I've navigated a world where pubs have been everything from hostile to welcoming.

I've never truly felt at home in a pub until I visited a desi pub – even though I only speak English and was taught to be culturally British by my parents. That's not surprising as all the venues in this book will treat you like a local whatever your background and wherever you're from.

Most of all, though, I'm truly honoured you've chosen me to be your guide especially if this is a world with which you're unfamiliar.

What does desi mean?

'*Desi is a feeling rather than an identity.*' CHEF KANTHI, Brighton (p80).

Despite having a father of Indian origin who was born in Singapore – which made him a desi – the word was never used in my childhood home in Dunstable, Bedfordshire.

My rootless childhood meant that we would speak English, apart from the occasional Malay word (my Mum was born in Malaysia) to describe food. This led to a huge ignorance on my part of India itself and South Asian culture. My parents would explain that we were British and different to other South Asians, which completely devalued their culture and led to my adult identity being confused.

I did hear the word 'desi' used when visiting one of my few friends of Indian origin in Luton, when their parents would ask for a cup of tea or curry made 'desi style'. The word has Sanskit origins – *desh* means land and country – but is most commonly used by people of Punjabi origins, although other Asians, such as those who have Gujarati heritage, are familiar with it.

Parminder Dosanjh at the arts organisation Creative Black Country, who produced a guidebook to desi pubs in the Black Country, explains: 'Desi means country, and in this particular case mother country.'

It can also be used as a catch-all term to mean Indians or even brown people – I use it this way to describe how a pub could be 60% desi and 40% white. Many Indians in Britain came via Africa, usually Kenya and Uganda, after those countries enacted policies of Africanisation (Idi Amin banishing Ugandan-Indians for example). Like my dad, and Lacki at the Ivy Bush in Smethwick, both of whom were born in Singapore, these people are desis, or even double desis if you like, as they often have multiple heritages.

'I started using the term "desi" after I moved from India,' says Gladstone regular Rachana Ramchand. 'In university in France we had events where we wanted to invite Indians, Pakistanis, Bangladeshis and Sri Lankans but we couldn't say all the countries, so we just said "desi".'

But the emotional aspect, as Kanthi says, is important too, and there's a sense of nostalgia attached to the word – a desi is someone who has left India or has family who have left the country. Indians living in India aren't 'desis'; they're influenced by the present, particularly the West (which includes films, video games, sport and even music), while desis are trying to preserve the culture of their homeland, even though that might be a culture from the past.

Coincidentally, I was expecting Ishaan Puri of White Rhino Brewery in India to be more familiar with the languages and culture in desi pubs than I was, but when I asked him to speak Hindi or Punjabi he said, 'I don't even speak Hindi to my wife, Dave!'

So how does this idea of preservation of culture manifest itself in desi pubs? Well, if you visit the Prince of Wales in West Bromwich you'll see a pub that some say is a 'proper desi pub', as if it's transported from India. But it's an India of publican Jinder Birring's memory from when he left the country. When contemporary Indians visit, however, they feel disoriented. A few even wanted beers served like in India – flat, with no head – but this was the Black Country and they were ignored.

In many ways this is the ultimate desi experience: the mixture of India and Britain, which has fused to create its own distinct identity.

Terminology used in this book

For nearly everyone I've asked, the term desi is inclusive, as used in the way Rachana Ramchand mentions on the previous page, but I should point out others do find it problematic, especially because it's commonly used to mean 'India', which could exclude all those groups from other countries that she mentions. However, it could also be used to mean pre-partition (pre-independence) India (or the Indian subcontinent) and this is how I use the term desi when referring to anyone of South Asian origin. I will also use the term 'brown' in this way.

Food writer and author of the *Philosophy of Curry* Sejal Sukhadwala used the term when she was growing up in India to mean something a bit backward or 'naff'. She and her sister would say a woman's makeup was a bit 'desi', for example. But most Asian people, particularly those of Punjabi origin, such as Nina Robinson, a lecturer at Birmingham School of Media, find the word more empowering. She even finds it unusual when white people use the term desi pub when 'it's the South Asians that have coined the term'. It is surprising, but we should cut them some slack as it's their way of navigating the post-racism world.

'I don't use the term white people a lot,' says Charu Agarwal, a desi I spoke to who lives in an area with a low proportion of brown people. 'I don't really see the world that way.'

But the term white people, as used by Robinson, will be used sparingly in this book, and only where it cannot be avoided. A good example of this is when I address the issue of 'authenticity' of the food on page 24. I've tried to use other words where possible because I know some feel uncomfortable with it.

The reason it's important to use all these terms is best explained by Jaspal Singh, an Open University lecturer who grew up in Germany with a father born in India and a white mother. 'People in Germany would find awkward ways of not saying I'm brown or Asian,' he says. 'It was an erasure of race because of what happened under the Third Reich. No one wants to be thought of as a racist and it took the murder of George Floyd for [German] people to start identifying someone by their race.'

It's hard to imagine us Brits as the grown-ups in the European room when it comes to anything, particularly race, but for people like Singh living in Germany it meant that no one celebrated his brown culture. And that's why it's important we use white, brown, people of colour (which is a catch-all term for non-whites) and black.

The latter is a reminder that in the past it was more common for Asians to identify as black. The best example of this is anti-racist campaigner Avtar Singh Jouhl (see pp18–19) who said: 'Many Asians don't consider themselves black, and some are offended at being called black. I don't want people who are oppressed and discriminated [against] being described as Asian. These people are black.'

So why haven't I called all South Asians black in this book? Perhaps because it would be confusing, but also this isn't how the Indian diaspora identifies in 2023.

'That started to stop,' says Jouhl's son, Jagwant, 'when ethnic categorisation was introduced and the politicisation of it disappeared. People looked at it in terms of the colour of your skin and not what your skin represents in terms of your political ideology or how your skin impacts racism.'

For people like Jagwant – and me, if I'm being honest – we're black in the sense we're fighting for justice for everyone who is on the receiving end of racism because we – and our families – have suffered so much prejudice. The racists might see us all as a 'not white' mass, and, in their eyes, the enemy, but that doesn't mean we shouldn't celebrate our distinct identities, whether that be British-Asian (me), British-Punjabi-Sikh or Gujarati-Kenyan-Indian. If we can have a hyphenated identity then we can be black *and* brown after all.

As a side note, West Bromwich Albion FC, which has a high proportion of match-goers of Punjabi descent and huge numbers of desi pubs near their ground, take the knee before kick-off. As I write this, WBA had just played Millwall at home and the symbolic anti-racist protest, associated with the Black Lives Matter movement, was met by booing from the travelling South London supporters.

The terms I avoid are sometimes completely personal to me, but I prefer diaspora to immigration or immigrant. My parents may have been born in the then-Malaya Peninsula, but they received a British education and all taxes my ancestors paid were handed over to the British. I am, therefore, not sure how you could describe any of my family or any of the people interviewed in this book as immigrants. We are all children of Empire.

This also informs how I use the hyphen British-Indian when other people will say 'Indian', as in that's an 'Indian pub'. The mark that colonials, particularly the East India Company, made on our lives means we culturally became British as soon as the pillaging and looting began. Looting wasn't even an English word (it comes from the Hindi lut) until India had its richness stolen from it – which shows that desi is one of a long line of words that have derived from India and been incorporated into English.

What is a desi pub?

The term desi pub was commonly used by British-Indians of Punjabi origin, particularly in the Midlands, according to Nina Robinson, who first heard it when she was growing up in the 1980s. But not all South Asians adopted it when they first started going to desi pubs or clubs.

Steve Sailopal, founder of Good Karma Beer Co, first started to go to the Century Club (p62) and Bollywoods in Forest Gate, East London, in the 1980s

Nina Robinson

and 1990s as 'these were the only places Asians could go without getting any grief'.

Steve Sailopal

Sailopal believes the phrase 'desi pub' gained prominence when local TV news stations got wind of the Indian diaspora setting up their own drinking spaces. They'd feature the 'phenomenon' through the white lens of newsrooms of the time, with a presenter venturing into a pub as if he was on safari.

It's hard to look back and say what the definition was as it's likely British-Indians, like Robinson, had a different definition to the presenter. Instead, we can look at how desi publicans and British-Indian regulars interpret the term in 2023.

'Desi means Indian,' says Lakhbir (Lacky) Singh at the Ivy Bush. 'You're going to an Asian pub.'

Put that way by Singh, it seems simple enough, but what if someone from Indian heritage became a bar manager at a Wetherspoons? What if a British-Indian guy opened a pub in an area that has no Asians and the only customers he had were white, serving them fish and chips with their pints?

I think we have to go one step further than Singh and say that a desi pub *is* an institution run by a person of Indian origin, but they also have to somehow stamp their culture on the boozer, whether that be through the food, music or decor.

Those of a more pedantic nature will wonder how my definition makes a desi pub different to a curry house. But even if you take away the bar setting, a desi pub is still vastly different to a traditional 'Indian' restaurant, because the food and service is very different.

First of all, there's the way the food is eaten. The curry house ritual – which in this country is forever connected with Bangladeshi chefs serving their interpretation of Indian food – is about catering to a post-pub crowd. By contrast, desi pubs offer a public house community setting where food can be ordered. Secondly, in a desi pub – as in any good pub that serves food – a customer who just wants a pint isn't valued less than a diner.

I don't want to diminish curry houses, but often they are linked to huge menus, food colouring and economical ingredients, whereas all the desi pubs I feature in this book offer meals cooked to customers' tastes with an emphasis on freshness. This isn't fast food. Last year in *Pellicle* I described the food in desi pubs as 'mixing the quality of high-end restaurants like Veeraswamy or Chutney Jane's in London with the accessibility of a curry house. It's top grub at pub prices.' I stand by this statement after visiting so many desi pubs.

I have met one Asian man living in a less than diverse area who told me – off the record – that a desi pub has to contain a majority of British-Indian drinkers: he thinks they should be brown-only spaces. But how do you define this? Is the Keg & Grill in Birmingham (p108) a desi pub only at night because it has a lunchtime crowd of office workers during the day? Is a Beefeater in the Black Country a desi pub because British-Indians drink there and are served by white staff?

Journalist Saptarshi Ray considers that view 'unnecessarily militant', but there is an exception that kind of proves my rule that it's solely about desi culture. It's a pub Ray used to drink in called the Three Horseshoes, which was in Southall, West London. It was run by Gerry Godbaz and was the only pub people would call 'desi', despite the landlord (from 2001–2004) being a white Kiwi. He wasn't any ordinary publican, however. He held bhangra nights while ensuring all his customers were included.

'What I loved about it,' says Godbaz (aka Gerry 'Singh'), 'was that it was an absolute melting pot: Indian, Pakistani, West Indian, older gentlemen from Somalia, Irish nurses. Probably the less frequent [customer] was [white] English. The bhangra music was a great success and kept our regular punters extremely happy.'

Godbaz shows that the best definition of a desi pub is perhaps a place steeped in British-Indian culture that fosters inclusion.

My desi pub history

There are two pubs I remember the most. The Crown in my hometown of Dunstable and the Blue Eyed Maid in Borough, South London. Both were firsts and both were memorable, sadly, for totally different reasons.

The first pub I ever visited as a drinker was the Crown. It was a horrendous experience and showed how difficult it is growing up in a white-majority town when you're a teenager. The pub in the early 1990s was very traditional, wooden floor, almost country-style (ironically, this is exactly the kind of decor I like) and filled with tobacco smoke.

I opened the door, the conversation stopped and then one person shouted. 'Anyone order a mini-cab?' There was a pause and then the whole pub, including the landlord, burst into laughter. The 'joke' was that anyone who is brown entering the pub would be a taxi driver and this is how they viewed all Asians. I ignored them and was served a pint of Wadworth's 6X. My love of cask ale started at 15 years old (photo ID-ing was rare then), despite the trauma of that first pint.

The subsequent years I spent in Leeds, London, Kent and Hertfordshire were a mix of pubs offering a very warm embrace and others where outright hostility was common. For every Barry Dennis, landlord of Sevenoaks' Anchor, who treated me like a family member, there was a Five Bells in South London, where I wasn't served after being told 'this was a Millwall pub'.

Then late one night in 2007 I found the Blue Eyed Maid in Borough, South London. It was the first desi pub I visited. The karaoke bar-come-

Indian restaurant was run by 'Jay' and his team of Asian bouncers kept things safe and were strong brown role models. Although the building's sign remains, it was a victim of the first lockdown. I haven't been able to find Jay and thank him for how he set me on this wonderful journey.

Luckily, round the corner the Glad (p68) was opened by the Khannas and I soon found my identity shift towards the Asian in the British–Asian hyphen. I love pubs and, finally, I could be myself in one.

The first desi pub

There are a lot of claims to being the 'first desi pub', including the Wheatsheaf in Coventry, which had a BBQ in the 1960s for visiting kabaddi teams. After rooting through newspaper archives, I think I've found the official first: the Durham Ox in Leicester, which was taken over in 1962 by Soham Singh.

I detailed its history when I visited the city to find the most notable desi pub and ended up at the Golden Lounge (p160). What's interesting about this post-war event was how the brewery at the time, Ind Coope, agreed to a desi landlord because the pub was 'frequented mainly by coloured people – Jamaicans and Indians'.

Singh had a white wife and was described by the Birmingham Daily Post as a '£30 a week crane driver' in the 'working class Gordon Street area of Leicester', which is near the city's Golden Mile. It shows that even in the early 1960s it was a job for hard-working British-Indians in traditional areas of cities and towns.

The Midlands had a culture of 'desi' social clubs opening alongside a few pubs, but the likes of Singh at the Durham Ox and the original landlord at the Red Lion (p148) faced hostility from fascist groups such as the National Front.

'When Jeet took over the Red Lion,' Parminder Dosanjh told me in an interview in 2021 for *Pellicle*, 'he was threatened and had regular visits from people saying "Go! You don't belong here. We want our pub back."

'Jeet often talked about having a baseball bat under the bar, and if he was faced by a gang, he would pull it out; not actually as an act of violence, but just to show them he was not threatened. He'd often say: "Come in and have a drink in the bar. If you're not pleased with our service, then you've got the right to complain. If you're happy, then stay and have a drink, but we want no trouble." So he had this really wonderful kind of noble approach as well as a warrior spirit.'

In London, from the late 1980s onwards, desi pubs such as the Century (p62) and the Regency (p44) offered safe spaces to British-Asians by opening with 'club' licences. This was because the authorities at the time couldn't understand why food and drink had to be served simultaneously. The ruling bodies also wanted to keep the communities separate, as Rahul Sharma at the Regency confirms, which shows how a ghettoisation approach was favoured over inclusion.

The most successful desi pub in the past was Southall's Glassy Junction which opened in the early 90s and was a raucous celebration of Punjabi pub culture. Saptarshi Ray frequented it and loved taking his friends there to give them a taste of how desi pubs were totally different to others in the area.

Glassy Junction. Photo courtesy of Ewan Munro, licensed under Creative Commons 2.0

'It seems sacrilegious that it's now a vegetarian restaurant,' he tells me. 'It was famous among Asians in this country but also in India. I was in Delhi and you'd meet people and they'd say: "Ah, Southall. Glassy Junction!"'

'It was famous because Indians could come and they could pay in rupees. The idea was you land at Heathrow, get picked up, get a pint and kebab without having to change any money.'

The fact that Southall could have a pub like this was cause for celebration as local bars like the Hambrough Tavern had hosted far-right groups who sparked violence, such as in 1981 when busloads of National Front members from East London entered the area and attacked shopkeepers. I was told about this incident by Gurlochan Brar, who drinks at the Scotsman (p75). He was aged 18 at the time.

'As the skinheads were walking to the pub,' he said, 'they spat at a little Sikh boy and he went home and told his brother. Word spread like wildfire, and the next thing you know it's all f***ing kicked off. The police tried to crack down on it but some guys [stole a] police van and drove it into the Hambrough Tavern and that's when it caught alight.'

Southall nowadays has two desi pubs of note (aside from the Scotsman, there's also the Terrace, p185), while the Hambrough lies derelict, with an application pending to convert it into a luxury tower block – which is fitting, because, as this book shows, it's easier to tear down racism rather than inclusive 'desi' spaces.

The colour bar

The reason desi pubs were needed was why Jamaican pubs such as the Angel in Brixton, South London, opened: segregation on the grounds of race. The experience I mentioned of being told 'this is a Millwall pub' a couple of decades ago was a common story for anyone of colour who wanted to have a drink in this country.

The colour bar operated by not allowing non-white people to enter premises, not allowing them to be served, and/or forcing them to drink in certain rooms, as was the case in the large pubs in Smethwick experienced by British-Asians such as Avtar Singh Jouhl.

In fact, whole tracts of social life were marred by this type of racism, as many interviews I have conducted show. Desi pubs had to be set up because of the experiences of British-Indians such as Nina Robinson's father, Balwinder, who was drinking in the Midlands and working in a foundry in the late 1970s and early 80s.

'[He] went to the Belle Vue pub [in Birmingham],' she says. 'It was white-owned and they used to go there all the time despite it being racist. They used to get a really bad vibe when they went in there and they used to give white people straight glasses and the Indians used to get the glasses with handles.'

Legislation in the 1960s should have made this kind of discrimination illegal, but it still continued, as these experiences showed. 'The informality of the colour bar,' says Kieran Connel, 'was maintained by word on the street. It didn't matter what the change in the law was because it wouldn't be wise to go to these pubs [as a person of colour]. Often these pubs would have strong connections to the far-right.'

In some areas, before desi pubs were set up, there simply weren't places for anyone non-white to drink in. Despite Handsworth, Birmingham, being a majority Asian and black area up to the 90s, it had openly racist drinking spaces, including a working men's club that famously had an all-white membership.

It was called the Handsworth Horticultural Institute (formed 1927) and operated as a typical working men's club familiar to anyone of a certain age or who has read Pete Brown's excellent *Clubland: How the Working Men's Club Shaped Britain*. It was a place people went to drink and play pool and darts, but, crucially, they were admitted only if they were members (the legislation passed in the 1960s exempted clubs).

'The situation was ridiculous,' Councillor Phil Murphy told the *Birmingham Post* in 1992. 'We had a black couple who were good friends with their white neighbours but only [the] white neighbours were allowed in the club. They could not socialise together.

'Members were left with the clear understanding that they must not introduce a black person if they wanted to stay members themselves.'

Eventually these clubs died out and you can read about how the Handsworth Horticultural Institute turned desi on page 100.

When I was researching the colour bar, I realised there was widespread ignorance on this subject. University-educated friends thought segregation was a US or South African issue, despite Avtar Singh Jouhl famously introducing US civil rights leader Malcolm X to a racist pub in the 1960s.

It got to the point where I had to scour old newspapers detailing hate crimes to create a Wikipedia page on the subject because a general page on segregation said it didn't exist in the UK. I also found that all these accounts were from the racists' perspective, with victims (or campaigners like Jouhl) rarely being interviewed. Although it's embarrassing to say that journalism is 92% white today, it was even less diverse in the past, which explains why more weight was put on white people's accounts.

Malcolm X in Smethwick

One question I keep being asked is 'what happened to the racists?'

'These working-class areas in the 1960s,' says Connell, 'were crucibles for multiculturalism but that's not to say these were happy-go-lucky places. There was a really strong strain of racism that took place. White flight is a part of that – the language used in inner city areas too, especially in the playground.

'The other side of the coin is that in the absence of the state it was left to the inhabitants of the inner-city areas to work out on a day-to-day basis what it meant to be an inhabitant of a multicultural inner city. That story is still playing out.'

Connell, who grew up in the Midlands, then details a perfect example of a post-colour bar world that should be celebrated. He's in a desi pub – the Soho Tavern (p116) – watching the World Cup final amongst Argentina fans, sharing a mixed grill and enjoying beers.

'This scene would've been unimaginable in Britain, certainly 50 years ago, but maybe even 20 years ago,' he concludes.

Avtar Singh Jouhl

'He had a cheeky grin about desi pubs. He'd think: "These were the places that didn't let us in and now we own them".' Jagwant Johal is speaking about his father, Avtar Singh Jouhl (their names are spelled differently because Avtar changed his surname to avoid his family being targeted for his activism in India), who campaigned against the colour bar in Smethwick when he first arrived in this country in 1958.

Jouhl, like many men from the Punjab, worked in the foundries and was fed up with racism in the factory, streets and, most importantly, in pubs. Unlike most of his fellow Punjabis, who were born in agricultural areas, he was highly educated – he originally planned to be a history lecturer – and was a communist, growing up in an Indian village that flew the red flag. But it was a visit to a pub in Smethwick, the Wagon and Horses, that sealed his fate.

He told oral historian Doreen Price, in a series of interviews conducted in the early 1990s, 'I opened the door and there were all white men. I asked why and they said, "Gaffer [the landlord] doesn't let us drink in that room," and we were allowed to only go in one smoking room and one public bar. I asked why and was told, "The gaffer says we talk very loudly and white people don't like us talking very loudly. And when we talk in Punjabi the white people complain that we are talking about them in our language." This was just the excuse, because in real terms it was the colour bar operating, and it was in every public bar in Smethwick and Handsworth.'

The landlords of the time would come up with a host of excuses to maintain this segregation and some said it wasn't a colour bar but a poverty bar. This was proved to be false as non-white doctors and teachers were not served in bars in the Black Country and around Britain. Near me in Lewisham, South London, the Dartmouth Arms famously barred a drinker, the mayor, when he visited with a black friend.

Jouhl was a member of the Indian Workers Association (IWA) and his comrades decided to take the fight to the racist publicans who had segregated white customers from their non-white counterparts, despite them working in the foundries together.

To do so he enlisted white university students to order drinks, then hand them to British Indians, such as Jouhl. The landlord would invariably eject them and then the IWA used evidence of these actions to successfully oppose the publican's licence when it came up for renewal.

Avtar Singh Jouhl (holding mic)

This led to some of the first-ever desi pubs in the country, and, decades later, the thriving multicultural makeup of Sikhs rubbing shoulders in bars with white football fans. Put simply, he's the grandfather of the desi pubs and the reason why Singh is such a common name for a publican. As he said himself: "You can play Indian songs here. It was not possible in a white pub.'

His protests gained national attention and led to US civil rights activist Malcolm X visiting Smethwick's Blue Gates where he proclaimed the racism to be 'worse than America. Worse than Harlem.'

Eventually the law had to outlaw segregation and it was Jouhl and the IWA's campaigning that led to the 1968 Race Relations Act, which banned racial discrimination in public places.

This was a huge step forward, but as Jouhl's – and my own – experience shows, racism was still a part of pub life. In the 90s he told of 'White men shouting "Taxi, taxi, taxi! Go back home, you fucking paki!" Even if you are a millionaire, they say, "You bloody paki!"'

Jouhl died last year, aged 84, and it is with sadness, and joy, that I admit this book wouldn't exist without his efforts.

The food

My father once invited a workmate for dinner when I was about eight years old in the mid-1980s. It was around the time of the 1986 World Cup in Mexico and this guy bought me some panini football stickers, including the foil England badge I had been coveting (it was later ripped up by my two-year-old sister).

When Ron arrived (I can't remember his name, but let's call him Ron) he gorged himself on tandoori chicken, naan breads and shish kebabs, all cooked on my dad's tandoor and BBQ he had erected in his garden. These dishes were followed up by deep fried fish pakora, lightly spiced okra fries and plates of fluffy rice.

Of course, none of these dishes were actually cooked on the day (apart from the rice) as no British-Asians had a huge clay pot, an outdoor grill or a deep fat fryer – especially considering our small kitchen – needed to make them. We did have a rice cooker, though, which I highly recommend.

The only way to eat these dishes would've been to go to an Indian restaurant (although delicacies like okra fries would've been hard to find then), but this is what Ron wanted. He couldn't believe we had chapati or roti instead of naan bread, and was also massively disappointed at the lowish heat levels of the chicken curry he was served (worth noting that I say 'heat' to mean chili, as I do throughout the book), and couldn't believe that we ate it on the bone.

Home cooking is always going to be different to eating out, and the types of food served will not be the same either. I'm not saying what my mum cooked was 'authentic' (a problematic concept I discuss on the next page), but she made Malaysian as well as Indian dishes. The Indian dishes she cooked were shaped by a mixture of inherited recipes, contemporary cookbooks, and ingredients available in the country at the time.

My mother was a good cook who was able to adapt and make loving meals. Because of that I pine for certain dishes (which you'll see versions of throughout the book) – particularly chicken wings, dals and rich curries. However, desi pub food is better than my mother's.

How could the food be tastier than someone who had so many visitors wanting to know how she cooked? Well, my mum wasn't a professional chef, and as mentioned, didn't have all the ingredients – especially spices, we had to take long trips to find these – and equipment to hand. (She once filled a suitcase with spices after a trip to Malaysia, which became infested with cockroaches when she opened it up at home.)

And here's a big confession – I never had a mixed grill until I visited the Red Cow (p130) for this book. As I explain below, they are as British as they are Indian, and although I've had all the components of the mixy before, I never had them cooked together on the charred bed of onions.

Desi pubs like the Red Cow produce amazing meals but are ignored by beer and food writers, maybe because they lack glamour, glitz and that dreaded word, hype. I also think class (as well as race) is an issue here: my contemporaries only feel comfortable in middle-class spaces.

Because of this I've not approached the guidebook entries like I'm a restaurant reviewer but as someone who is highlighting the best dishes to eat in the country. This doesn't mean that I've consistently put the food front and centre – I believe this book needs to be a necessary voice for the landlords, kitchen and bar staff, and the regulars – but there are times when I just fancied talking about a curry (such as when I visited the Spice Rack Lounge in Stanmore, North London, on page 49).

The first gastropubs

Here's a question: how does a pub become a gastropub? The first 'gastropub', the Eagle in Clerkenwell, North London, details on its website what set it apart from other pubs at the time it opened in 1991. It states that before they came along pub food was 'rubbish' because of the way pubs were owned. The Eagle based their food on 'big flavours and rough edges', and this spawned a recipe book that wanted to end 'pretentiousness and over-complication'.

This sounds to me very much like a desi pub. 'Gastro' isn't a term many desi publicans feel comfortable using, but maybe this is a good thing because in gastropubs I don't feel that comfortable as a drinker or even a casual diner/drinker.

Gastropubs came to my part of London when gentrification crept in, and black and Asian drinkers were made homeless again. This was because they were being priced out of boozers rather than being subject to the colour bar. This is why the Wetherspoons near me is the most inclusive pub in the area and why gastropubs lack diversity.

In other parts of London and the Midlands plenty of pub goers have been enjoying the 'gastropub' experience in desi pubs without knowing, especially after the smoking ban meant pubs such as the Red Lion could make dining such a pleasurable experience, in a more inclusive environment.

(cont. p24)

Mixed Grills

For Jack Spicer Adams it's the lamb chops. For Neel Joshi it's the lamb shish kebabs. For Nina Robinson it's the fish pakoras. And for me it's the wings. Everyone it seems has a different way to 'attack the stack', but what we all agree on is how special a mixed grill is and how well they suit desi pubs, offering communal, spicy sharing.

V's Punjabi Grill (p95)

If you're never had one, a 'mixy' is usually a combination of marinated meats and fish (vegetarian versions are fairly common) cooked in a tandoor, and then 'sizzled' on a grill (usually a gas stove) after being doused in lemon juice. They can be served in all sorts of desi pubs, but they offer one key ingredient that other boozers selling traditional pub grub can't: theatre.

When a sizzling platter is brought through a pub: everyone stops and stares. It pauses conversations and I remember being in Gravesend, where the Canal Tavern (p95) doubled as a vaccination clinic, and a queue of pensioners looked on in awe as a series of mixed grills were being brought through.

Unpicking its origins is a tricky task. I asked Lakhi Singh at the Ivy Bush in Smethwick, and he told me: 'Mixed grills are meat cooked in a tandoor. Back in the day in India or Pakistan they used to cook it in the ground. You're cooking meat through flames and they're through skewers. The prawn [pakoras] are cooked in a pan though.'

A tandoor was an invention that made its way from India, but the mixed grill has as many roots in this country as it does in Asia, according to Sejal Sukhadwala, food writer and author of The Philosophy of Curry.

'Mixed grill,' she says, 'is a British concept. It comes from a mixed grill in Britain where you'd have lamb chops, sausages and chips. And this is an Indian adaptation of an English mixed grill.'

V's Punjabi Grill (p95)

Confusingly, the rural Ivy Inn (p89) calls its mixys 'sizzlers' because its mainly white customers would mistake them for the traditional version served in Spoons or Harvesters. Even more perplexing is that the nearest approximation to a mixed grill in India is usually called a sizzler.

Ivy Inn (p89)

'Sizzlers in India,' adds Sukhadwala, 'are strips of meat or stuffed vegetables, you get some rice, you get some chips, some baby sweetcorn, grilled tomato and that's all cooked on a hot tawa [a versatile cooking pan]. It's different from the mixed grill you get here and it's quite retro food as it was huge in the 1980s and 1990s.'

Sukhadwala mentions chips, and in this country it's potentially a divisive North (or Midlands) v South issue, with Londoners finding it odd that a mixy in Birmingham or the Black Country must come with chips.

'When I went to Birmingham,' says Joshi, 'they'll always get masala chips and I didn't understand this. We went to the Covered Wagon with my mate TJ and his uncle who was from Birmingham and he ordered them.

I personally wouldn't because I like having naan bread with them.'

Chips aside, mixed grills are hugely popular with families on a budget as they allow members to share. They are also one of the many elements that makes a desi pub so diverse.

'It's cheap,' says Robinson. "A large grill will feed a family of four. It's difficult now though as rising costs have increased these grill prices.'

The question everyone asks is, 'where's the best mixed grill?' I'll let Spicer Adams – who I've seen attack the stack – answer that.

'The Grove in Handsworth [p100],' he instantly shoots back. 'Head and shoulders above the rest. The onions at the bottom are vital, it's that mix of flavours from the soft sweet bits alongside those acrid black, burnt, crusty patches. You have to scrape them off the bottom and there's a real satisfaction in getting down to the last scraping.'

As Spicer Adams says, from top to the very bottom, a mixed grill is the perfect pub grub, satisfying us in so many ways.

Glassy Junction (p189–190)

The gastropub is obviously a media term and people may have differing definitions of it. It also has a class element – similar to the bottle shop/off-licence – that somehow elevates it above other pubs. One definition I did note with interest on the Eagle's website was about how beer choices had to be decent, which did make me chuckle as my nearest expensive – but hugely popular – gastropub stocks multinational-owned 'macro' lagers but no cask beer. I talk about the booze on offer at desi pubs later, but it seems that a lot of gastropubs like the term but not the Eagle's original mission statement.

Perhaps then it's best we don't call desi pubs 'gastro' as it's such a problematic term to get to grips with.

Authenticity of food

Sometimes you have to use the phrase 'white people'. Although it can be divisive and uncomfortable for white readers, there are times when the description is apt and unavoidable. This is one example: white people always ask me which desi pub has the most 'authentic' dish, and I find it a question that is unanswerable. So much so I often bat it back and ask 'what exactly do *you* mean by this?'

To get to grips with this I've spoken to a few experts about the idea of authenticity, and it's easy to see why I'm fed up. The concept is mired in colonialism, stereotyping and cultural misconceptions. So, let's start at the beginning and look at why people – who are always white – ask this question.

'You have this section of white people,' says Jaya Saxena, food writer and correspondent at eater.com, 'who want to get it right and be respectful but they almost overcorrect and start chasing this idea of authenticity which is largely a myth.'

The chasing of authenticity that Saxena mentions is what I find most off-putting as it becomes a competitive pursuit that denigrates entire dishes. For example, butter chicken, a staple that many British-Indians, like me, love.

This dish exists because of colonialism. We're not just talking about the foreign intrusion into India by the East India Company's ships, but other civilisations' influences too. So it's easy to see why the idea of authenticity is deeply anachronistic.

The butter chicken we eat today has many ingredients which wouldn't have been 'authentic' to India. Tomatoes, the base for our curry, were introduced by the Portuguese, as were chilies (Mexico via Portugal). And as for the chicken and butter … how far back do we go to be 'authentic'?

'In India there were no chilies until the 16th century,' says Sejal Sukhadwala, food writer and author of *The Philosophy of Curry*. 'There were no potatoes or curries till the 18th century – so would you say the real authentic food is the one without chilies, potatoes or curries? Where do you draw the line? I think the word authentic is very problematic.'

The food in desi pubs is filtered through the Indian diaspora and that diaspora, like my mother's cooking, was affected by the produce available at the time of their arrival.

There's a scene in the sci-fi series *Torchwood* where visitors from the turn of the century arrive in our modern world and are amazed at the produce offered in a Sainsbury's. My mother, who once had to eat water spinach – a weed-like green – in Malaysia all winter, felt similar feelings to the time travellers when she came here in the 1970s.

'When you come from a culture which associate meat and dairy with luxury, you're going to change your diet,' Saxena says. 'If you can buy dairy every day and meat for the same price as most vegetables that does change what is "authentic" and what is "home cooking".'

My mother's cooking, for example, was based on meals that would never have been served in a village outside Kuala Lumpur, but which now appear in Malaysian restaurants. It's not that she was one of those *Torchwood* time-travellers, but there were cookbooks that interpreted Malaysian foods to include meat, like beef rendang, a coconut-y, dry curry.

In the case of desi pubs, chicken tikkas, etc., were created by the diaspora, and many of these dishes were eaten simultaneously by British-Indians and white British people for the first time. So, when it comes to 'authentic' British-Indian dishes, you've probably had a fair few of these already in curry houses, street food joints or takeaways.

If you want 'authentic' Indian food, however, then that's even more problematic, even if you jump on a plane. As India was being changed by colonialism it didn't stand still. Those leaving their homeland looked to where they had gone to for inspiration: the West – the US as well as Britain.

Friends in India tell me of mixed grills being sold there called 'British Sizzlers', and they do the same with the curries we are all familiar with. 'They have chicken tikka masala on the menu,' says Sukhadwala, 'and they bill it as British-style curries.'

The idea of authenticity is, therefore, very difficult as we live in a globalised world, with mass consumption of movies and TV shows. This has led to some cultures being valued over others. For example, why do high-end restaurants offer fusion foods featuring Japanese or Scandi cuisine when the greatest example of fusion food, desi fare, is so ubiquitous?

'I find the definition of fusion food so interesting,' says Saxena. 'Every food could be fusion. Really, we're talking about race: the immigrants from Japan and Scandinavia were often wealthier.

'Given the colonial relationship with Britain and India: there's still this association that this is a cheap food of a lesser culture.'

It's not. And I hope this book proves that. But one question lingers: why do some desi pubs advertise authenticity themselves? It's common to see 'authentic Punjabi cuisine', for example, especially because it turns out that the Punjab has one of the highest concentrations of vegetarians.

'It comes from wanting to assert your identity,' says Saxena. 'If you're a member of a diaspora, you're in the minority and facing discrimination. Or you don't have access to all the ingredients or touchstones of culture then there is a defensiveness of "we're going to build this. This is ours."'

And it's not just Indian food culture where this happens. Saxena tells me about New Yorkers trying to find the most 'authentic' meatball spaghetti, when Italians wouldn't have eaten this dish in the past.

Perhaps, though, it's easy to be overly critical when white people are offering an opinion on these kinds of foods. When someone says 'this is a really authentic pakora' they're really just praising it. After all, these conversations must show how Indian food (in Britain) is a huge cultural phenomena.

'It's a signifier to the extent to which Britain has become multicultural,' concludes Kieran Connell.

Women and desi pubs

After interviewing so many British-Indian landlords for this book a few trends have emerged. The most telling is the aptness of the gendered term 'landlords', because, as far as I know, the only 'landlady' is Megha Khanna at the Gladstone, in Borough, South London. Compare this with all pubs nationally, where one in three licensees are women.

Despite this disparity, Meg throws herself into the role, and runs the bar with her brother Gaurav, but she's also an outlier, as desi pubs were traditionally male spaces.

The other common theme is the number of desi pubs that have been set up by those who came, or had ancestors, from the Punjabi region of India. Without lapsing into stereotypes, it's fair to say that they have a strong drinking tradition – one that is easy to romanticise because they had the determination to carve out safe havens.

In the era when British-Indians sought to find safe spaces to drink and set up their own pubs (from the 1960s onwards) misogyny was rife and the first desi pubs weren't an exception to this. They – like all drinking establishments back then – were not natural family spaces. There were exceptions, like the Century Club in East London (p62) which included families and women when it opened decades ago.

Nowadays, of course, this has changed, and the bad old days of the uncles sitting at the bar passing judgement on women has been eradicated – at least in the establishments I've visited.

However, when I put this to food writer Sejal Sukhadwala, she says I'm not in the position to comment about desi pubs being female-friendly because I've never experienced the feeling she's had when she's entered a desi pub that has a majority male clientele. And, of course, she's right.

Nina Robinson, a lecturer at Birmingham School of Media, grew up in a family that had a strong (male) Punjabi drinking culture. The very first desi pub she went to was the Grove in Handsworth, before it was refurbished in the early 2000s, and on page 100 she talks about how it went from being all men to very family friendly.

Nina says the earliest desi pubs in the West Midlands were the social clubs, like the one her father, Balwinder, used to go to in Walsall, which opened late and was full of men of Punjabi heritage drinking hard.

'The women,' she says, 'would have bloody good fun. They'd be a samosa production line and at weddings I remember being stuffed in rooms with so much singing and dancing.

'The men were the boring ones drinking. We'd be having proper fun – telling lewd jokes and making up lewd rhymes.'

Shivani Kenth is married to Ajay, who runs the Tap & Tandoor mini-chain and has set up a street food restaurant in Moseley called Zindiya. She has a hand in the T&T's running and what she tells me about old-style desi pubs resonates with Robinson's experience. Kenth's father drank with other men in Spark Hill Social Club on Friday, despite it being next door to a community club frequented by the whole family.

'As a kid,' she tells me, 'we couldn't even go to the door to see our dads.'

The issue of representation is key to this. Kenth is a visible, friendly presence at the T&T in Solihull, but Zindiya takes up most of her time and prevents her becoming a notable publican for the area. She is a trailblazer to me, though.

'The key to unlock the desi pub success is how well they cater for women or how comfortable women feel there,' Nina adds. 'What I want to see next is a Punjabi landlady. That's the only way we're going to have proper change.'

The best person to speak to, therefore, is the only landlady of Punjabi heritage I've found and that's Khanna.

'When I told my friends,' the 36-year-old says, 'that I was taking over a pub. They were like "oh, my God, you're going to be a landlady!" but I didn't even know what that meant. They were like "you're going to be like Peggy Mitchell!"'

Meg Khanna

'Now, it feels like trendsetting to be a young landlady, as well as an Indian landlady.'

I ask Khanna if she experienced any hostility visiting desi pubs like the Prince of Wales in Southall, and she says this wasn't the case. Unlike pubs in Dartford, in Kent, where she has a flat.

'People [in Dartford] do look at me in a strange way when I enter the pub. But I think that's to do with being a woman going alone to a pub which is a completely different thing.'

The Khannas grew up in Zambia, in southern Africa, with parents she describes as open minded, so they didn't have any objections to her running a pub. In fact, her words echo Robinson's, especially with how the drinking culture has recently revolutionised – and not just for the diaspora but for older Indians in India.

'On my mum's side,' she says, 'it's pretty traditional, but they've changed a lot. There was a time when the men would drink on Fridays and they would close the doors and be on their own. The women weren't allowed to drink or even go into that room.

'Now that I work in a pub my uncles and aunts have become very open about drinking. They want to get their children involved more, especially now they're older. It's interesting that you asked me about this because I've just been to my uncle's place and we went out for dinner.

'We were in Amritsar [a city in Punjab] and it was bring-your-own booze. My uncle bought me some wine and asked if my [female] cousins wanted to share it. They've modernised.'

As the desi pub owners have modernised so too have the boozers. Places like the Red Lion (p148) might be male-owned but they cater for all types of families – even those with autistic children – and know their success depends on it.

Beer and desi pubs

When this book was announced it was met with widespread praise that an underrepresented area of the beer world would finally be given deserved exposure to a wider audience. And whenever I've written about desi pubs, readers get in touch saying they want to visit one straight away after discovering small tasters about their culture, history and mixed grills.

But there are always doubters, whose comments usually take the form of 'why is an institution like CAMRA being involved in a sector of pubs that serve so much lager?' Well, here's something that may surprise you: remember my first ever pint at the Crown? It sparked a lifelong love of cask beer and a scepticism of lager, which I find too carbonated for my digestive system.

With some very notable exceptions, desi pubs don't have a range of drinks that would excite real ale and craft beer lovers. The reasons why are hard to unpick, but the main one is the way that beers such as Cobra have been marketed.

The British beer (said to be Indian) was launched by founder Karan Bilimoria in 1989 to be a perfect pairing with curries or other dishes with plenty of heat. It was said to be smoother, less gassy and 'quite unlike any other beer'. 'What was special about Cobra?' says Steve Sailopal. 'Everyone [believed the marketing] and used to say: "You don't want a beer that bloats you: have a Cobra." It was a load of bollocks and Cobra got away with it.'

In fact, as others explain elsewhere in this book, a pale ale might be the best choice for a curry as the subtler tones pair nicely with the different flavours.

But maybe it's wrong to judge desi pubs by their beer range and look at why they serve the beers they do as there's obviously a customer demand for the likes of Cobra.

'Price point is very important,' says Gaurav Khanna at the Glad. 'If you take Southall [West London] these beers would've been what their customers had been drinking when they were growing up. I would say what defines a desi pub is more the food than the alcohol.

And when you're out of central London there's only so much you can charge for a pint.'

Crafty Indian (p168)

There do appear to be changes happening though, with the Regency (p44) serving Rothaus and places such as the Indian Brewery in Birmingham (p104) serving more interesting beers. It doesn't take a lot to change a bar to have a more varied range, as Khanna has shown in the Glad, which has so many amazing beers – including cask ales.

There's a reason why Khanna has travelled with me to a few desi pubs – they transcend their beer range and offer different experiences. So, put aside any scepticism you may have about CAMRA supporting the 'wrong' type of pubs, because while beer might not come first, community certainly does.

Cost of living

It's a bit of an understatement to say we live in turbulent times. During the production of this book there was a lot of disruption to how pubs operated due to a series of events including train strikes, Covid restrictions, recruitment difficulties and a World Cup that had kick-offs at unfeasibly early times.

All this meant that publicans had different concerns as I progressed with the many interviews. But one unavoidable event started to loom large towards the end of our conversations and that was rising energy and food prices. At the time of publication this hasn't led to mass pub closures, but it has manifested itself in how desi pubs have conducted their business. Put simply, desi pubs have become less profitable as the owners absorb the rising costs for fear of losing custom. When I spoke to Kalpesh Amlani at the Purple Flame in North London, who once ran numerous pubs, he admitted that it's the wrong time to expand because he is subsidising his customers so much, having only raised his prices once.

I tend to err on the gloomy side when it comes to the current economic situation, but I do think this is an unsustainable business model. I really recommend you try as many as possible of the pubs I've mentioned because you might find that what you're holding in your hands transforms from a guide to a history book.

London

Aroma Lounge

96 Llanover Road, North Wembley, London HA9 7LT
T 0208 904 5432
aromaloungeuk.com
Mon–Thu 16.00–23.00; Fri 16.00–00.30; Sat 12.00–00.30; Sun 12.00–23.00.

Wembley is a place synonymous with football. The iconic stadium looms over the area, casting a shadow over all the businesses. What's forgotten, though, is that the borough of Brent – where Wembley sits – is very diverse, with a British-Asian population of over 35% and growing. Because of the football ground, it's a place often travelled through with scant regard for the pubs in the area, which is a shame, especially as it has quite a few desi pubs.

The best of these is the Aroma Lounge in North Wembley, which is full of (desi) football fans watching live games, especially when Man United or Liverpool are playing.

When I take friends to a desi pub for their first time I get all types of reactions – they're always positive and sometimes unexpected. The most common response is amazement that a pub full of British-Indians would be thriving under their noses. Maybe some people think these kinds of pubs are niche when, really, they're success stories that welcome brown and white people alike. Whatever the reason, today's reaction was euphoria.

Amir Dehghan's parents escaped Iran after his dad was arrested for trying to organise a trade union. They settled in Newcastle. Amir eventually studied art at Goldsmiths in South London and worked in numerous craft beer institutions in Lewisham. We became firm friends when he served me (many) craft beers at a local pub and I enjoyed talking to him about our favourite breweries – an eclectic mix of Harvey's, Beak, Villages and Burning Sky.

One day I told him about desi pubs. 'What's a desi pub?' he asked incredulously. A few weeks later he entered the Aroma Lounge in Wembley, on a night when Liverpool lost to Man United – much to the annoyance to the majority of the pub's clientele.

Shiba Tiwari (left) and
Dharmesh Vaghela (right)

For a while he couldn't speak, totally overawed by the food and the atmosphere, but most of all by being in room full of brown people. It's not that Amir ever felt threatened or even uncomfortable in the pubs in our area; it just becomes the norm that you're an anomaly and different to others.

In the Aroma Lounge Amir was just another face in the large crowd – it was the first time he'd felt like that in this country. Everywhere he's lived in the UK, from Newcastle to Lewisham, has been tolerant of him, but this new experience was celebratory – strangers greeted him warmly before he said a word. I saw his face as he walked in – a mix of contentment and bemusement – and on the Tube home he couldn't stop enthusing about how he had always craved this type of experience.

Of course, it might have just been the food. There's a strong argument that co-landlord Shiba Tiwari might be the best chef in the country. That's right: not the best desi pub chef, nor the best chef of Indian food, but the best chef full stop.

It's a bold claim, I know, but here's my compelling argument (I hope). There's nowhere in this country where you can get such high-quality desi, pub, vegetarian or restaurant food cooked (or overseen, as there's a team of chefs as well as Tiwari) by someone who really wants to push the boundaries of excellence.

Just naming the dishes makes me hungry. Mock Duck is cooked in a gravy sauce that is delectable, with the soya chunks deep fried so they hold

Aroma Lounge

Shiba Tiwari

firm and feel truly meaty. Tiwari tells me they're marinated in black pepper, white pepper, and salt, then deep fried and tossed in sauce with green peppers. It's a cliché, but in this case it becomes a truism, that everyone, especially vegetarians or vegans, will ask 'am I eating meat?' They're not sceptical or complaining – it's simply great food.

This isn't the only exceptional dish on the menu. There are tandoori chops of such delicate spicing that it feels a shame to wash your hands afterwards. I tend to eschew red meat for health reasons, but when you couple these bad boys with the mint sauce it feels like you're holding the best roast dinner and spicy meal in the palm of your hands.

And then there's the mixed grill. Usually this is a cholesterol challenge, but the Aroma's is so pleasurable, so expertly cooked that eating it becomes a mindful experience, to be savoured slowly. Normally, I would have been watching the football with everyone else, but this was a sizzling distraction of joy and I became entranced with the food.

Tiwari runs the kitchen so that Zambian-born Dharmesh Vaghela can run the bar. Service is very swift – there are even buzzers you can press to get your drinks if you don't fancy the short schlep to the bar.

When they first opened the Aroma Lounge, they didn't really publicise the venture as Tiwari had been working in Indian restaurants for 27 years and they knew his food was so good it wouldn't need any slick marketing. 'With a pub,' Tiwari says, 'you have sport, you have good food, you have nice beer, you have entertainment. It's everything you want in one place.'

But it was a struggle at the start. Wembley – because of the stadium – has some of the toughest parking restrictions in the country, which meant they had to rely on local trade, especially as they weren't advertising the opening.

'It took six months,' says Vaghela. They gained a loyal following from Facebook groups such as 'CARBDashian', which may have a ridiculous name but was great resource for me in finding where the best mixed grills were up and down the country. The word of mouth worked. Now 95% of their customers are 'desi' and they have nights like the one that took Amir's breath away.

Despite being a few miles from Wembley stadium, they do get some footballers drinking in the pub. I'm reliably told that a few Tottenham Hotspur players even come here. The biggest draw for groups isn't football, though, it's Koroga, a style of southern African cooking from Vaghela's homeland. A large BBQ metal plate is placed outside the restaurant and customers can cook their own curries. It's for large groups only but harks back to the heritage of Punjabi foundry workers in Smethwick cooking their own food outside places such as the Red Cow (p130) in the 1970s.

It's all part of a unique experience that sets the Aroma Lounge apart. You might think of Wembley only for the football stadium, but when you've visited the Aroma Lounge you'll soon link the area with one of the most diverse dining and drinking experiences Britain has to offer.

And if you're anything like my friend Amir, it could be a very emotional occasion too.

Mixed grill at Aroma

Boulevard Sports Bar

15 Friern Barnet Road, Southgate, London N11 3EU
T 0208 368 2200 · boulevard.uk.com
Pub: *Mon–Fri 17.00–23.00; Sat 13.00–23.00; Sun 12.00–22.00.*
Kitchen: *Mon–Fri 18.00–22.00; Sat 14.00–22.00; Sun 13.00–21.00.*

Southgate in North London is equidistant between Arsenal's Emirates and the Tottenham Hotspur Stadium. Therefore, I expected the Boulevard Sports Bar to be a battleground of boisterous male football fans, knocking back pints as one side revels in the other's disappointment.

I support Arsenal because of how safe I felt as a young football fan of colour visiting Highbury, Wembley and then the Emirates, but all football fans can annoy me. I was in a pub about five years ago in the North London when some Arsenal fans started chanting a song that was both anti-semitic and racist. When I told them to stop, I was shouted down.

So, when I reached the Boulevard on a Friday night and saw the blacked-out windows, I took a deep breath before I walked in. To my utter amazement it, though, it was like watching *The Wizard of Oz* when the film switches from monochrome to glorious technicolour. The pub's interior immediately quashed my prejudices, and I was confronted by all types of people sharing different experiences in a relaxed community setting.

There were women at the bar. There was a white middle-class family explaining the dishes to their teenagers. There was a group of desis celebrating a birthday. There were pensioners – brown and white – enjoying their food. And all this wholesome merriment was being marshalled by the very avuncular figure of Kalpesh Shah.

It turns out there are many community occasions here: quiz nights, WhatsApp support groups formed during lockdowns meeting regularly; sports teams; local business meetings; the list is endless. And the reason is Shah, who grew up in the area and went to the same school as many of his customers. His story, and the Boulevard's, mirrors the post-racism settings familiar to anyone who has visited Smethwick's Red Cow (p130) or Blue Gates (p123).

Kalpesh
Shah

Boulevard Sports Bar

Shah is now 53 years old and came to the UK when he was aged six. Southgate then was mainly Irish and Italian, and he lived in nearby Finchley. He was surprised by the prejudice he experienced in the playground.

'Initially I didn't know what the racism meant,' he says. 'I was born in Kenya and schooled there. In Kenya everyone just got along with each other whether you be black, brown or whatever – we'd all visit each other's houses. It was only later that I found out what the names meant.'

Shah's family moved out of the area and he worked in commuter towns around the M25/M1, like Watford and Hemel Hempstead. You'd be forgiven for thinking his childhood experiences would have put him off returning, but the opposite was true, and he took over the pub in 2010 when one of the founders died.

'When they [the racists] were kids,' he says, 'it was what they had been taught. Or what they watched on TV. But they've since grown up in a mixed culture, had diverse friends and realise [they were wrong]. Someone who was racist will now come with an Asian friend or a black friend.

'It's funny, as the bullies and racists at the school are our regulars here. They had to change.'

The area doesn't have any pubs like this and some of the punters rely on it as a lifeblood. I strike up a conversation at the bar with Debbie, who has become part of the pub's family. She loves the atmosphere Shah has created. She also attended the same Southgate school but a few years after Shah.

Tarka dal

She tells me, 'I can't imagine life without this place. I would be devastated if it closed.'

The bar is so busy I have to operate in a backroom, which means I incur the friendly banter of a family who watch me take photos. They have interesting jobs, such as acting, and I overhear one mention they're friends with the musician Goldie. Despite coming to this place for a long time, the first time they came across the term 'desi pub' was a few weeks ago when artist Grayson Perry was filmed visiting the Red Lion in West Bromwich.

You can be immersed in desi culture without realising. I extol the virtues of West Bromwich, and they don't see it as being different to London. It is different in that much of the capital is very ghettoised, but maybe they're right in a way. If your experience of London is the Boulevard, then it must feel like the city is truly integrated.

This type of inclusion is a source of pride to Shah, and that sets him apart from other desi pubs, such as the ones nearer to Harrow, whose clientele is more skewed towards British-Indians (though a lot of that is due to demographics and not the publicans, who welcome everyone.)

My food comes and it's wonderful. Shah is a Hindu and his family were originally Jains, who usually eschew any plant that grows under the soil: no potatoes, onions or garlic in their curries. He admits this 'had to go out of the window' when they arrived in Africa.

The dishes that are served are very different to other desi pub fare: lots of delicate vegetarian ingredients cooked expertly, but meat fans shouldn't worry as there are still plenty of sizzling platters.

The standout is a Gujarti delicacy called Patra made from Colocasia leaves, which Shah says are often used for plates in South Asia. I've seen this done with banana leaves in thalis (which means 'platter'), but Colocasia leaves are new to me, and offer a taste of India (and Africa) that I'm not used to.

The Patra look spectacular, like cut-up, marbled Swiss rolls, and despite being deep fried, feel wholesome, with a spice that packs a secondary punch. I'd say they're perfect as a shared starter or as a grazer to have with your beer. I can't imagine I'm the only one who has discovered a love of them.

A parade of dishes then followed the Patra, which were equally as magnificent. The chili prawns were huge, in a light batter, drenched in sauce but still remaining crispy, and perfect with naan and dal. The tandoori wings were lightly charred and had competing flavours of spice and light yoghurt marinade (these are too moreish to be shared, so be warned).

So, is the Boulevard red, like Arsenal, or white, like Spurs, I ask Shah.

'We have more of an Arsenal following than Tottenham,' he admits. 'But when it's the North London derby you'll get half and half. It's really good banter going on, it's exciting. But it's not just men – you have families coming out to watch it. Everyone locally finds this place a safe haven. It's a friendly atmosphere and everyone's eating and drinking.'

I might have just found my safe space to watch Arsenal play outside of the Emirates, but everyone will like this place, whatever the occasion, and I implore you to try it. You just have to look past the exterior and embrace the warmth inside.

Tandoori chicken wings

Purple Flame

437 Honeypot Lane, Stanmore HA7 1JJ
T 0208 204 2380 · purpleflamelondon.com
Pub: Mon–Fri 16.00–22.00; Sat & Sun 12.00–22.00.
Kitchen: Mon–Fri 16.00–22.00; Sat 12.00–22.00; Sun 12.00–21.00.

Metroland was the name given to suburban areas of Buckinghamshire, Hertfordshire and – most pertinently for this entry – Middlesex. The enduring phrase was coined by the Metropolitan Railway's marketing department in 1915 for a 'Metro-land' guide aimed at commuters looking for homes.

The poet laureate John Betjeman was the 'hymnologist' of Metroland, with an influential TV series inspired by his 1954 collection *A Few Late Chrysanthemums*. To others, though, north-west London was suburban hell. Writer and columnist A. N. Wilson said: 'No wonder, when war came, that so many of these suburban prisoners felt a sense of release.' Metroland's capital was said to be either Harrow-on-the-Hill or Wembley, but today, I think the most fitting centre would be either Stanmore or Queensbury.

This area of north-west London gets criticised for being car reliant, with too many multiple-occupancy properties that are falling into disrepair. But scratch beneath the surface and the dullness of the suburbs, which Betjeman detailed, seems to have been banished, with British-Indians queuing up to buy sweet- (or tobacco-) filled paan leaves, going out to late-night clubs, or dining out in style in the area's many desi pubs.

A lot of these Asian pubs were founded or run by the Purple Flame's Kalpesh Amlani who co-launched the Regency (p44) with his brother and Navin Sharma, introduced a DJ to the Spice Rack in Stanmore (p49) and made the Honeypot in Honeypot Lane a safe space for desis. His empire may have dwindled to consist solely of the Purple Flame, but he had a hand in moving this part of 'Metroland' away from humdrum housewifery into a hotspot for desi culture.

The Purple Flame is not a fading last stand, however. It has a lovely, family-friendly vibe, unique dishes and a publican who knows his stuff.

Amlani's first business was opened in 1982 with his brother Nilesh (who now runs desi club Trilogy in Edgware). It was called Queensbury Video and Paan shop – now a minicab company next to the Tube station – which allowed the brothers to buy the nearby property which would become the Regency.

The brothers invited Sharma to join them as he had successfully run the desi Premier Club in nearby Sudbury, but they were only allowed to open if customers signed up to be members. The Purple Flame – which was previously called Symphony – also had to be a members-only affair when it was set up 1994. Amlani took it over in 2012 and changed the name.

'Navin and I were partners,' Amlani tells me. 'And we opened the Regency together. It started as one unit [it's now massively expanded] and it used to be purely men – you never saw women. Then it got a bit modernised.'

There must have been a sense of solidarity among Sharma and Amlani because both were exiled from East Africa, the former leaving Kenya in 1971, and his friend leaving Uganda a year later. Jomo Kenyatta and Idi Amin's policy of Africanisation led many Asians to be exiled and follow similar paths.

Sadly, the bond between the two was broken and Amlani doesn't even know if his photo is still hanging up at the Regency, like other former co-workers, despite it being a only short walk from where we're sitting. 'We fell out,' he admits. 'After 19 and a half years. Unfortunately, we're not talking. It wasn't very nice between myself, my brother and Navin.'

Purple Flame

Aloo

The night I visited, Amlani appeared later in the evening, despite the bar staff telling me I've had a wasted journey. I watched him work the room while the football played on TV and the grills sizzled.

Amlani is the type of publican that causes his customers' faces to brighten as he remembers their family and the good times they've shared. I tell him about my book, and when I ask him for a chat he says 'of course' and I'm given instant access to his world – the ultimate privilege – where every question is answered truthfully and thoughtfully.

It turns out that he's a self-taught cook and recently started experimenting in the Purple Flame's kitchen. The name, by the way, has no real meaning: 'Four of us sat down and just started bombarding words.'

The dishes I chose were purposefully different from other desi pubs. I'm coming to the end of the adventure and variety is important, otherwise you'd think only mixed grills and curries are on offer. I have Methi Gota with onions – round potato balls with a dry spiciness that demonstrate the chefs' skills with heat, potato and chili – 'Aloo' (a great side dish), and 'Atomic chicken', chicken pieces on the bone cooked in a fiery red chili sauce. I tell Amlani that it was super hot and addictive, making me want to keep at it despite the heat.

'That's why it's called Atomic chicken,' he laughs. 'We've got different levels: chili chicken, green chili chicken and Atomic chicken.'

The crowd at the Purple Flame are mainly desis on the evening I visit, but there's a mixture of white people, young and old. Amlani says that football is popular – Liverpool are a big team here – and cricket if it's the World Cup.

He has a core of regulars who come most days for drinks. They'll watch Test Match cricket if it's on, but they're really here because it's a community hub and Amlani is a superb custodian. He keeps the flame alive.

But there are two notes of sadness when I speak to Amlani. The first is that his partner at the Purple Flame, Sam Desai, died at Christmas, aged only 44. 'It was tragic,' Amlani says. 'He was with me for 27 years. He was a barman at the Regency from 17 years old.'

The second sadness is his shrinking empire. Amlani says it's the wrong time to expand because rising costs means profits are a lot lower. The prices of ingredients keep rising – so much so that he's basically subsidising his customers (a common theme when I've spoken to desi landlords recently). He's already had to increase his prices once and if he does it again then footfall will be affected, despite having a range of core regulars who visit most days.

I ask him what it feels like to start so many businesses and give so many people a chance in the industry. He answers: 'The best thing is the buzz.' Which may surprise people who are expecting this part of London to be a sleepy backwater. In fact, I'd say it's the place to be. It's positively buzzing.

Purple Flame

Methi Gota

Regency Club

19–21 Queensbury Parade, Edgware, Middlesex HA8 5NR
T 0208 952 6300 · regencyclub.co.uk
Mon 18.00–22.00; Tue–Thu 12.00–14.30, 18.00–22.00;
Fri & Sat 12.00–15.00, 18.00–22.30; Sun 12.00–22.00.

Before I start my chat with Regency Club owner Rahul Sharma I notice what I think is 'smoke' coming out of a fruit machine – a surreal image in the otherwise perfect vision of a beautiful desi pub. There's no reason to be alarmed, though; this 'smoke' is actually an integral part of the whole experience.

'To create a certain ambience we use incense sticks,' says Sharma. 'We had a special fragrance created because ambience isn't just about décor, seating, music – smell plays a big part as well. Smells can take you back to certain places. We've created one that complements the heritage we've built here. My parents are from Kenya and migrated here [in 1971].

Pankaj Rana

The spray has sandalwood, vanilla, cloves. It gives you a sense of spice as you walk in, as well as that sense of prestige of walking into a members' club.'

The incense prepares the diner for the aroma from the kitchen and Sharma claims it complements both morning and evening smells. The bhuno cooking process (see p50) means that at the start of the day you'll smell onions being fried and then later on meats being barbequed.

It seems that every detail, from the Regency's raised bar – which Sharma says creates 'a theatre' – to the old-fashioned signage, via the stained-glass dome is purposefully curated to whisk the customer to pre-independence Kenya. Creating a unique olfactory experience is the logical next step. This enticing aroma emanates from the bustling, wooden-shack-style kitchen, where the chefs (14 are employed in total) are working hard to produce the high-quality Kenyan food which is cooked with Indian spices.

The Regency is not only one of London's best desi pubs but one that's managed to keep its former community feel, as well as offering plush dining. Sharma's father, Navin, who is now aged 70, opened it in a former car parts shop in 1991, alongside Kalpesh Amlani and his brother Nilesh, with the intention of creating a safe place for desis to drink in. At that time non-white customers weren't being served in many of the pubs in the area – 'they were racist,' admits Sharma.

His father previously had a desi pub in Sudbury called the Premier Club but the council would only agree to the licence if it was a members' club rather than a space to serve all of the community (it's interesting to note that in those days licencing ghettoised drinking rather than embracing diversity). Nowadays, Navin has taken a step back from the business and Sharma runs it, which has led to this recent spectacular refurbishment (though the pub's founder remains a constant presence).

'Working is in his blood,' Sharma says. 'He's our PR guy. He comes in and says "hello" to everyone. We know the third generation of our customers we serve them day in day out. We're part of the community. It's not just business we support each other all the time.'

On my second visit I'm greeted by first name by the uniformed staff. The dress was part of the club's heritage and was more retro – dare I say garish – in the days before it became the tasteful, modern version after the revamp during the Covid pandemic. The yellow and black ties that the staff wear are a lovely touch and show that the Regency Club is more than a desi pub – it's a brand.

'What we found pre-Covid,' Sharma says, 'is that Wednesday and Thursday used to be more corporate days. Because we're on the Jubilee Line people would come from Canary Wharf and we used to give members' ties to a lot of our customers. They'll go to work with their Regency ties and then all come here with them on.'

Sharma, who is a qualified pilot as well as holding a degree in business management, may have been given the choice to take over from his father when he was aged 21, but the Regency brand he's created wasn't just something bestowed on him. Because of the family nature of the business – his dad was often joined by his mum in the kitchen (some of her recipes from the 90s are still used) and his uncles worked here too – he feels that he has a duty to keep the Regency thriving.

'I never wanted to be that person,' he says, 'who was just given something to run. I thought of this as a platform to build on and not a business to run day in and day out. I started washing up in the kitchen – I worked there for a couple of years. I worked my way up: crying my eyes out chopping out onions. Do you know how many onions we go through? Then prepping, the grill, waiting and then the bar. In the beginning I used to work 120 hours a week.'

During this period Sharma describes how basic the Regency was compared to today, with orders taken with a pen and paper and customers having to wait more than two hours for a table. Booking online is something we can take for granted in 2023.

The path he describes, from bottle-washer to front of house, was undertaken by a lot of desi pub landlords: for example, Abhi Paudel of the Fishponds Tap in Bristol (p83), who Sharma used to work with. You can even see some of these people in the photos on the wall, along with some of the waiters when they were (a lot) younger.

The influence of the Regency can be seen in a lot of desi pubs in London and beyond, and it's not a hyperbole when Sharma calls it an 'academy', especially as all the desi pubs in the surrounding area are run by ex-managers, ex-waiters or ex-chefs.

I list all the elements that I love about other desi pubs to Sharma to see if the Regency can match, or better them: the home-made sauces of the Fishponds Tap (yes, they do that too), the old desi regulars you get at the Scotsman in Southall (snap – they even have their drinks ready when they see them arrive outside on CCTV).

But there's one selling point the Regency seemingly lacks: the jumbo naans at the Scotsman. 'Our naan is about that big in size,' Sharma says. 'And then we cut it into pieces and bring it to the table. If we made one naan at a time we couldn't feed the amount of people we do.'

Since Covid the food business is now 40% takeaway, so you can see why putting too many demands on those working the tandoor oven would be an issue. But it was the pandemic that showed just how community-run the pub was when Sharma made the decision to help key workers. During lockdown they made thousands of meals to send to hospitals, homeless people, charities and those stuck at home.

Ironically, it was the strange decision to make the Regency a members' club rather than serving the whole community in the 90s that paved the way for this type of work.

'This was supposed to be a home away from home,' Sharma says. 'For a lot of the immigrants it was sleep, work, sleep, work. This place was escapism. Somewhere they could go to hear Bollywood music. People would walk in and feel every time that it was a reunion and it had that social club feel to it.

'Everyone was drinking and we thought "let's serve some food as well". The food became very popular, so people came not just to socialise but to eat as well. Which allowed us to expand the pub and eventually buy four shops.

Mogo

We're not allowed to expand more because the landlord said we've got a monopoly in the parade.'

The club licence still operates. During Covid it was tweaked to allow families to dine, apart from Friday and Saturday nights, which are restricted to over 18s. It's archaic, but like a lot about the Regency, they've made it work.

I thought this would be the ideal place to bring the landlord of a Sussex pub one midweek day for his first experiences of a desi pub. He was amazed by the venue, the food and the atmosphere – England had just lost to Pakistan in the cricket and there was a great mix of sports fans, diners and drinkers at the bar.

'We do a dish called garlic mogo,' Sharma explains to my guest. 'It's cassava boiled, then it's deep fried, crisp on the outside, soft on the inside. Then it's wok fried. It's a very traditional Kenyan-style dish, it's one of our signature dishes and we sell 36,000 portions a year of it. You'll always see it on every single table. It's really snacky.'

We order this first and it sets the tone for the rest of the meal, with my friend claiming, 'take this to any pub in the country and everyone would love it'. And in one dish that's how I feel about the Regency – any of its elements can be transported to another pub and they would be universally adored. But like the sandalwood smoke, once mixed with all the other flavours it creates one desi pub experience you can't forget.

The uniforms, the smells, the food – it's a truly intoxicating mix. But I'm not going to make any food recommendations. There's no point. When you decide to come to the Regency you've already made the only decision that matters.

Spice Rack Lounge

35 Church Street, Stanmore, Middlesex HA7 4AR
T 020 8954 6374 · spiceracklounge.com
Pub: *Tue–Fri 12.00–15.00, 17.00–22.30; Sat 13.00–late; Sun 13.00–22.30.*
Kitchen: *Tue–Fri 12.00–15.00; Sat & Sun all day.*

When I was planning the research for this book, I thought it would be sensible to undertake the project methodically, whether that be town by town or from south to north. This would ensure I covered all the pubs I needed to without a mad rush at the end to visit far-flung places. But this approach failed to take account of my mood and the need to visit a specific desi pub because I'm craving the comfort of a particular curry – a desi chicken curry.

The day I visited The Spice Rack Lounge in Stanmore was during the sombre period when huge numbers of people from around the country queued to visit the Queen lying in state. I had been visiting desi pubs in West Bromwich when her death was announced and was moved by how important she had been to other people. In every desi pub the TV would be switched from Test Match cricket to coverage of the Queen's death without any complaints, even from ardent Indian fans wearing their country's colours.

I also was recovering from a virus when I visited the Spice Rack and needed the restorative, nostalgic hit of spicy food, plush surroundings and desi hospitality. Just walking through the door was comforting in itself, the room immediately filled with multi-coloured beams of light from the massive stained-glass domed ceiling, beckoning me into this cathedral of curry.

The building used to be a post office, but in recent years has undergone a remarkable transformation into a very striking establishment with a long bar, exposed lighting and comfortable soft furnishings – the type not usually associated with desi dining. It first became a pub 15–20 years ago, before changing hands to the current owner, and it is now a very popular nightspot for the many desis in the area.

In the day, it's one of the most relaxing desi pubs you can visit, with a lovely, sedate atmosphere that becomes livelier during football and cricket

matches – if you're planning on going on a weekend then you do have to book. Stanmore may have been a long trek for me – the length of the Jubilee line and two buses – but it has a village feel that makes the trip worthwhile. This could be a rural Kent village with cosmopolitan cafés rather than a London outpost.

The Spice Rack's plush interior is not reflected in its prices. They even have lunchtime deals including a starter, main, naan and poppadoms for around £12. This meant I could order chicken fry (an Indo-Chinese dish) as a starter and the desi chicken curry as a main. This curry – often appearing on desi pub menus as village-style chicken curry – is based on a dish that's sold in Dhabas (roadside restaurants) in India where customers include truck drivers and travellers looking for food that reminds them of home. This is quite apt because whenever I order this dish it takes me back to Saturday nights of my childhood when we were allowed to eat in front of the TV, dipping roti into chicken curry.

The food is cooked bhuno, which is a Hindi word describing the entire curry-cooking process of sauteing (the onion base), stir frying and stewing (the meat). When cooked roadside (and in desi pubs) the curries have a lot of ghee added, giving them a comfort food quality, and the initial stages of bhuno are done at a high heat to give it a smoky flavour. The curry I had at the Spice Rack had a small amount of tempering, which is a topping of chilies and ginger fried in (more!) ghee. Despite the use of so much ghee, I'd argue this is the perfect food if you're feeling down or even ill.

The medicinal use of chicken curry makes sense if you consider the ingredients that go into it and the way it's cooked. Some experts claim that chicken soup is like penicillin, and they could say the same for chicken curry as it's also similarly stewed and slow cooked. The scientific part is the way the bones break down into the broth (sauce in the case of curry), releasing gelatine, glucosamine and chondroitin which help repair tissue and reduce inflammation. Add to this the onions (which contain immune-boosting phytonutrients), garlic (antimicrobial) and ginger (antiviral), and it becomes the perfect cure – or prevention – for any virus.

Furthermore, the spices used can be very good for someone recovering from a virus. Turmeric is ideal for stomach pain, and cinnamon and chilies work wonders on sinus pain. Chilies can also give you a lift if you're feeling down – the release of endorphins is similar to going on a run, and I know when I need a mental health boost that eating chilies really helps.

But the biggest health benefit for me – as in all the desi pubs I've visited – is that this is a safe space where I can be myself. This might sound fanciful but numerous studies have shown that people of colour not feeling welcome or having to suppress their culture can have an adverse effect on their health – both physical and mental. And when I left the Spice Rack that day there was a bounce in my step.

Clockwise from top right: chicken fry, desi chicken curry, rice and poppadoms

Sun & Sand Lounge

16–18 Hendon Lane, Finchley, London N3 1TR
T 020 8346 0580
sunandsandlounge.com
Mon–Fri 17.00–23.00; Sat 15.00–23.00; Sun 15.00–23.30.

One of the many delights of visiting as many British-Indian pubs and bars as possible is sharing these experiences with people who are new to the culture. In North London the heritage of desi pubs differs from the rest of the country as it's not Punjabis but Hindus running the show. Well established lounges and bars like this one in Finchley, set up in 1989, had to operate as members-only clubs to gain a licence to sell alcohol (as was the case at Boulevard in Southgate, and the Purple Flame and Regency both in Queensbury).

So, if you're visiting from the US, and are unaware of this history, like my non-binary friend Holly who tags along today, then things can get a little confusing. 'I thought we were going to a pub,' they say. Because at first glance, the table seating, the service, the greeters, and the way the food is served points towards this being a restaurant. However, when I pointed their attention to the bar to observe a distinguished gentleman of Punjabi heritage sitting quietly eating nuts and drinking a beer, the community pub-like nature of the Sun and Sand Lounge became apparent.

Jaggi Singh Litt is 65 years old and came to Britain from Malawi in 1975. He studied accountancy in Manchester but when he moved to London he loved the various desi bars in this part of the capital, especially this one and another called Marina. Sadly, the founder of the Sun and Sand died when he was very young – from a heart attack in his 50s – and Litt misses him to this day. Litt may have Punjab origins but must have felt comfortable here because of the bar's links to Africa.

The current owner Haree Patel's parents were from East Africa (Kenya and Tanzania) and so was the previous owner. 'That's shown in the kind of food we have here,' says Patel, who took over from the sons of the founder.

'A lot of these places [in North London] are set up by people who came

Sun & Sand Lounge

Jaggi Singh Litt

over from East Africa, so the menus are quite similar. The lamb chops, the tandoor dishes – they've got a Kenyan or East African twist to them. That's the attraction of the food.'

Vegetarians here love the paneer, while meat eaters love the lamb chops and kebabs. The non-meat dishes in particular are put together with a lot of thought because Patel himself is a vegetarian: 'I concentrate quite a lot on the vegetarian menu,' he says. 'People always say you've got a nice, extensive vegetarian menu.

'When I was young, all my friends ate meat. When we went out it was sometimes a struggle to find something. It was a bit of a challenge. But now this menu is great.'

Despite older male customers' love for the Sun and Sand under its previous owners, it was failing to reach a wider base. It needed a massive refurb and Patel describes the red decor, fabric seats and facilities as 'quite bad'. The other issue was that the members' licence made growth tricky.

'The problem we had,' he tells me, 'was because it was a members' club – and this is from conversations I've had with people who used to come here – it was very gentlemanly, very focused on males. Maybe once a week they'd have their wives turn up.

Chili garlic mushrooms

'The blacked-out windows [a feature when these clubs were set up], were uninviting and passers-by would think it was a strip club. You couldn't see in or out and it had "members' club" on the outside and people were like "what's going on in there?"'

It made sense for Patel to change the windows first, but it wasn't easy as they were oddly positioned – the building was once a Portuguese fish restaurant with the catch of the day displayed so people could see it from the street. The other problem was the toilets which were 'disgusting', according to Patel.

'I got rid of the male culture by spending a lot of money,' he says. 'Where it was all dark and gloomy, I brightened it up quite a bit. I modernised it, opened it up and now people could see in and out. We then focussed a lot of our energy and service on making families feel welcome. I wanted a place where you can confidently take a date you're trying to impress!'

Which wasn't part of my plan when I took Holly. The food we ate did impress, though, especially how it managed to be both light and substantial – which is a fitting metaphor for the Sun and Sand in general. The heat was prominent, but not in a way that drowned out the subtle spice flavours.

We ordered mock 'not chicken' Karahi (marinated soya pieces in a sauce), which didn't have a fake meat texture and was more like paneer or tofu. The fish masala curry was rich and tomato-y, while the standout dish was the aubergine Orro which was hearty, satisfying and held together with an almost butter-like texture.

The two sides chili paneer (soft texture, but with a nice firm bite) and chili garlic mushrooms (super crispy, decadent almost) were also highly impressive, showing off the considerable skills of the chef. Patel tells me how each dish is road tested by him and his friends numerous times before they're unleashed on the public.

A few older customers might blanch at the way the Sun and Sand has changed, but on a Thursday night it was brimming with all different types of customers – young, old, white, brown. What I was most impressed with was the range of food being ordered, with mixed grills being brought through with all the theatre you'd expect, as well as vegetarian dishes cooked to Jain standards (without anything grown under the ground, such as onions and garlic).

The popularity of the rejuvenated Sun and Sand shows that inclusivity is a good investment.

Chili paneer

Tamil Prince

115 Hemingford Road, London N1 1BZ
M 07988 750721 · thetamilprince.com
Bar: Mon–Fri 12.00–23.00; Sat & Sun 11.00–23.00.
Kitchen: Mon–Fri 12.00–15.00; 17.00–21.30; Sat & Sun 12.00–21.30.

When people hear I'm writing a book on desi pubs the one place I'm most told – and told is the most apt word here – to go to is the Tamil Prince. The type of person who makes this 'urgent' recommendation is usually someone who has never visited a desi pub but reads restaurant reviews and likes to whitesplain.

I also sense a bit of metropolitan elitism in people on Twitter telling me about a new place in Islington, when desi pubs in the Midlands have recently opened (such as the Tap & Tandoor, p133) that nail the gastro side of the business. To me a desi pub is somewhere that contains all types of social classes, where you don't always have to book, and which can be used as a relaxed boozer. For others, controversially, you can't be a desi if you're of Tamil origin, as explained in the book's introduction.

But maybe I shouldn't be so dismissive, for there's a certain amount of inclusivity in popularity. On my visit here there's a 50% mix of people who could be deemed diverse, and I'm seated next to two desi women celebrating a birthday. Most tellingly, there are lots of personal reasons why I should love this venture by Indo-Malaysian basement pioneers Roti King.

Travelling the country visiting pubs run by landlords of Punjabi and Gujarati heritage has been a cultural learning process as my parents were Singaporean-Indian on my dad's side, and Malaysian on my mother's. The foods they cooked were similar to the fare in desi pubs, particularly the 'dhaba' chicken curries, but a lot of dishes have been new (and highly memorable) experiences.

My mother's roti canai is a cherished childhood memory, and naans – which I do love – are inferior in comparison, so the Tamil Prince's familiar selection of dishes is the nearest I'm going to get to these memories.

As someone who has queued up at Roti King, it's refreshing to dine in a relaxed, and simple but beautifully decorated small bar area. The staff made me feel special and I forgot I was on a production line of customers – 30 covers at lunch, 80 in the evening and 200 all day on Saturdays and Sundays.

They recommended a Harbour Brewing Company Daymer Extra Pale to go with my okra fries and the citrus-y beer dovetailed nicely with the crispy, lean snack. The second starter I had (the portions are small, especially as they're meant to be shared) were chicken lollipops – they're fiery heat-wise but soft and crispy, reminding me how my mother used to fry chicken in a wok.

The paneer curry I had next was rich but not oily, despite a blood-like deep gravy, cooling down the palate after the chicken and as invigorating as any chicken curry that I've eaten. It's food that can end any lingering meat cravings.

Then we get to the roti. It makes me cry with nostalgia because it's so much like those of my childhood, rich with dairy (my mother made hers with condensed milk and egg) and perfect with the paneer.

I realise I was wrong to misjudge this place. Perhaps that came from inverted snobbery towards anything popular. The Twitter experts were right to recommend it. It was an emotional visit, having my childhood comfort cuisine served to me at a bar, and it shows how lucky I've been while researching this book that so many different experiences have been gained by such vastly different cooking. Part of me, though, yearns wistfully for this kind of food but in a more humble setting.

Three Falcons

1 Orchardson Street, St John's Wood, London NW8 8NG
T 020 3868 6741 · threefalcons.com
Pub: *Mon–Thu 12.00–23.00; Fri & Sat 12.00–24.00; Sun 12.00–22.30.*
Kitchen: *Mon–Sun 12.00–22.30.*

Edgware Road is synonymous with Arabic hospitality, and I've been a big fan of its many restaurants that line this major West London throughfare in the decades that I've lived in the capital. Give me a kebab, sit me next to the mangal (the open barbecue) and serve me a beer and I'm more than happy, especially in the colder months.

I've never thought of it as a particular good place for pubs, though, but if you walk towards St John's Wood then this assumption is not just banished but exploded.

The Three Falcons plugs this gap and much, much more, though very few people know about it. The reason for the cloak of anonymity is Google, which lists it as a hotel (it has a few luxury rooms above the pub). Because of this I was expecting the sterile air of a lobby, and functional food with little character eaten by a transient population.

The Three Falcons may be unkown to most, but it's not much of a secret to the many desis who live in St John's Wood and enjoy the plush surroundings, beautiful food and warm atmosphere. You'd think this was overseen by an old hand steeped in desi culture but I think Zora Singh may be the youngest landlord in the country at 20 years old. Singh's talents flow from his father, Bobby, who is a restauranteur in Delhi.

'My father's so passionate,' Singh says, 'that he's bound to do well. I look up to him and he believes you have to go against the tide to make it.'

Delhi-born Bobby was the one the one who found the pub when he was with his friend Lucky, who was born in the UK. It wasn't anything special in those days and Singh describes it matter-of-factly.

'It was really rough,' he says. 'But the price was really good for a pub with two floors that could be turned into a boutique hotel.'

'Rough' is a word that I wouldn't use now, but the then-Richmond Arms did have a feel of a traditional wet pub that hadn't had much money spent on the interior. It's easy to be sniffy about such community pubs, but when Singh shows me photos of what the bar looked like it's fair to say the investment was needed. It wasn't 'rough' in terms of clientele but it had a shabby appearance.

'It was a mess,' he says. 'Now we have customers who work at Lord's, like the head coach of the nets. Varun was born in India and he visited when we opened in the beginning of 2019.

'He used to come when it was the Richmond Arms buying fish and chips and scampi. But now he loves the Indian food, especially the fish Amritsari.'

The dish Singh mentions is particularly good with beer as the fish is cooked in gram flour, spices and herbs. A friend from Mumbai reckons it's even better than anything he can get 'back home'. Which kind of makes sense. The food I talk about in this book may have originated in India, but the ingredients are, in general, fresher here, with higher standards. The food in the Three Falcons appears simple, but is lovingly crafted and presented.

The curries are definitely on the pricey side compared to most other places listed in this book, but are reasonable in Gastropub terms – a chicken Chettinad, for example, is £17, but is a gorgeous blend of 12 spices and slow cooked so the meat is super tender. The seafood dishes are also worth trying.

One highlight that marks it out from other desi pubs is the desserts. The Gulab Jamun Cheesecake dressed with Rose Petals and garnished with pistachios is a sweet delight that will banish any reservations some people have about Indian desserts. (I think this notion comes from the fact that a lot of Indian pastries and cakes are less sweet than the kind of biscuits, tarts and puddings found in Europe).

The menus – which are made to look like an old *Delhi Times* newspaper – are fascinating in themselves and explain Indian history through its famous landmarks.

'My idea with the menu,' says Singh, 'was to keep the customer engaged. If they're too big you get bored or confused. When I went to restaurants in five-star hotels when I was younger with my dad, they'd be 200 dishes. They want to do everything.'

Singh's dad runs a restaurant in Delhi called Wok in the Clouds which is very famous for its murgh makhani (or butter chicken). This popular dish, in the UK and India, originated from Delhi's Moti Mahal restaurant – a place that claims to be the first in Peshawar to introduce tandoori chicken after they dug a tandoor in the middle of the restaurant.

'A lot of the recipes are very similar [to a Wok in the Clouds],' says Singh. 'But the butter chicken is the exact same recipe. It turns out a lot of people say our butter chicken is better than the one we have in Delhi because the produce here is better.'

You would think this interconnection with Delhi means it's a pub for desis, but you'd be wrong. The crowd in the Falcons is very mixed and changeable – when the cricket is on TV it can tip towards India, but on other days it's just like any other pub in London. And also being a hotel means that the pub's population is more transient, bringing a different experience with each visit. I've been here when it's very desi, when it's very white, and, on occasion, when it had an Arabic feel (Morocco were playing in the World Cup).

Singh should be proud of what he's achieved here. Having an excellent menu and serving so many members of different communities is the best 'hype' you can hope for.

Fish Amritsari

Century Club

454 Romford Road, Forest Gate, London E7 8DF
T 020 8472 1701
Tue–Thu 17.00–23.00; Fri 17.00–01.00; Sat 15.00–01.00; Sun 15.00–23.00.

The best way to get to know how an area has changed is to delve into the history of one of its long-standing pubs. Until relatively recently the East End of London wasn't a safe place for the South Asian diaspora, and pubs were no exception. Steve Sailopal, founder of Good Karma Beer Co, grew up in the area after being born in Bow in the 1980s, and when he reached drinking age, he found pubs to be hostile environments for non-whites.

His father, Lachman, had the same problem in the decades previously. The only place he could find that was safe to drink in was in Epping, Essex, where a woman ran a pub that wasn't hostile to British Indians. Lachman would drive (or be driven by family members) to this public house dressed in a suit, seemingly undaunted by the length of the journey time. Here, in the heart of the Essex countryside, he would order pints of bitters and whisky chasers and find a haven away from a hostile city.

But for Sailopal this wasn't an option and he found himself hoping that one day he could drink in a safe place and just be himself. Luckily, in 1988 Kenyan-born Hindu Peter Patel (his birth name is Pankaj but prefers Peter) set up the Century Club in Forest Gate. Peter's experiences of drinking in South and East London chimed with Sailopal's.

It all started at a Croydon laundrette in the 1960s, when Peter was just 12 years old.

'In those days everything shut at 5pm,' he says. 'The laundry would open until 9pm. Next door was a pub which had a piano, and I was always fascinated why everything was closed and this pub was open.

'Through a swing door I could hear people laughing and see them smoking, drinking and enjoying themselves. I thought: "I want one of these when I grow up."'

Hitesh Joshi

As well as this childhood memory, it was a later visit to a Lewisham pub with friends that made Peter decide he should open a bar that would serve desis like him. During that visit another customer purposely spilt his drink on Peter, claiming he had tripped him up, and demanded more than another drink as recompense. The atmosphere turned ugly, but the publican sided with the aggressor and the Asians were kicked out, despite already having spent £40 (the equivalent of £300 today).

'It was a lot of money as a pint used to be under a pound then,' Peter says. 'We did nothing at all. That's when I decided we needed something for Asian people. Not many Asian people went to the pub – it was mainly white people. When we went most people were alright but one of two wanted to pick a fight.'

However, licences were only given to wet pubs and Peter wanted to serve Indian food. When he applied, the relevant authorities said the venture sounded more like a restaurant.

'Indian people,' he says, 'Don't want to go to the pub and have a curry afterwards when the pub is closed. They want to eat with their drinks.'

There was an example in London of an Indian bar being given a licence and in the end he was able to open the club in 1989 after obtaining a bank loan. The popularity of the Century – at the time very few bars like this existed in the country – meant people travelled from places like Brighton to visit.

It was also a very family- and women-friendly, inclusive environment – which was rare for desi pubs at the time – and Peter would cook food like chicken tikka and shish kebabs. There was no menu, but his small kitchen was always busy, offering his punters bespoke dishes which he lovingly prepared.

The only problem was that Asian gangs would target businesses, trying to extort money after vandalising property. Peter's answer was to involve the police, not just by calling 999 but by finding a way to get plain clothes officers to protect the building in exchange for being fed and watered.

'I wouldn't say it was organised crime,' he says. 'More a bunch of thugs getting money off the Asian businesses.

'The boss would send all of his lackeys in and then would come down to my club like he's not associated with these guys. He'd say "Give me £500 or £1,000 and I'll make sure they never come down again." But I'd been living in East London since 1972 so I knew what the score was.'

'In the Indian criminal world,' Peter adds. 'We were known as a police pub.'

The pub was a hub for many Asians, particularly Hindus, and wasn't as raucous as other establishments that were set up as safe havens for British-Indians who didn't feel welcome in traditional pubs. Having a culture of women and children customers meant there was no trouble, and the policemen really enjoyed their shifts.

'Everyone wanted to work the nightshift at the station,' he says. 'In fact, the Century got such a good reputation with the police that they used to hold their leaving dos there.'

This novel approach guaranteed the longevity of the bar and Peter remained custodian for 30 years until his wife got sick and competition from other desi bars and pubs became fierce.

Today, the place is owned by Mukesh Kanbi who has totally revamped the interior and made it sleek and polished. The atmosphere is more relaxed but the food – cooked to order – is worth visiting for. Kanbi admits to me he took the place over so he could keep it as somewhere the uncles could meet to exchange stories of the old days, and a place where he could host business contacts, as well as playing cards with his mates.

We order a few staples. I particularly enjoyed the tandoori prawns from the menu. Kanbi tells me I can order what I like, something that might not last when they start to publicise the place and attract more punters.

It's also a great place to watch sports and I visit during a Premier League match and get the chance to speak to some of the punters who have enjoyed coming here for decades.

'This was the only place in East London,' explains Hitesh Joshi, 57. 'Available to Asian people at the time and they used to queue to get in, especially at the weekends.

'You name [an Indian dish] and he would cook it. There used to be music too. The location hasn't changed, but the layout has. It's a lot better now, a lot more modern. The bar deserves to be known and have a better reputation. It should attract crowds at the weekend like it did in the past.'

Joshi's first proper pint was here and today he's visiting with his son Neel, who is one of the most knowledgeable people I've met when it comes to the nation's desi pubs. The continuity of a father and son loving this place shows how family friendly it was, and remains today, and illustrates the enduring appeal of desi pubs for the next generation.

'My first beer was a shandy in Cornwall,' Joshi says. 'But my second beer was here. Not only do I come with my son now, but I brought him here with my missus and my daughter when they were quite young.'

The Century is an under-the-radar place – secret almost. Kanbi likes to keep it ticking over for business meetings and as a bar where he can eat great food. But that will change when he employs a bar manager who can publicise it more.

In the meantime, enjoy the food and savour being part of its rich history of being the UK's first desi police pub.

Tandoori prawns

Crown & Pepper

242 High Street, Croydon CRO 1NF · T 020 8688 7507
32 Godstone Road, Caterham CR3 6RA · T 01883 212222
crownandpepper.co.uk
Mon–Thu 12.00–23.00; Fri & Sat 12.00–24.00; Sun 12.00–22.00.

Croydon has a recent history of desi pubs. The Windmill catered for all types of drinkers, including Crystal Palace fans during home matches. Sadly, though, it had to shut as the building has been sold.

At the other end of town is the Crown and Pepper, whose success inspired the Windmill to open, and which is so well regarded that another branch was opened by owner Raj Shukla seven miles south in Caterham. Those living south of the river who bemoan the fact that desi pubs are 'too far' should realise they have these two – and the Glad (p68) – in close proximity.

It's easy to make false assumptions about both Crown and Peppers as they have large menus and sell Chinese and Indian food. The reality is they're large operations and have different chefs for each cuisine, which actually makes a lot of sense considering the number of Indo-Chinese dishes on offer in most desi pubs.

The idea came about after Shukla visited the Regency (p44) and struck up conversations with other pub goers who had travelled a long way. 'You'd find people there who were coming from South London,' he tells me.

'I'd ask them why they were here and they would say "there's nothing in South London". This pub [in Croydon] came up and I grabbed it. When we started, we had a lot of Indian customers and locals would come in for the sports and see the sizzling lamb chops.

'It's not like a normal restaurant where you're sitting down. Here you're watching football with a pint and suddenly someone's walking around with a plate of kebabs.'

When I visited the Croydon pub a few months ago there was scaffolding up as the frontage was being redesigned and a new private lounge was being built at the back (which should be finished by the time this book is published). So, I decided to visit the Caterham pub instead.

Where the Croydon branch caters for a post work crowd and sports fans, this bar felt very local and was heart-warmingly busy for a Wednesday evening. The town has a lot of Fuller's pubs, so I was pleased to be served an excellent pint of London Pride, which went down smoothly with my dinner. My dining companion, who lives in the local area, says this is by far the best pub in the town.

Food wise I put the Chinese chef to the test by trying the mogo (cassava), which was cooked in a Szechuan pepper sauce. It tends to make food very zesty – perfect with a pale ale – and usually my palate struggles with the heat, even though most people find it mild. It's not a spice that I was accustomed to growing up, but here that's not an issue as it's lightly sprinkled into the sauce.

It's not a huge departure to have Szechuan in an Indo-Chinese dish as it's a key component of a five-spice mix found in chili chicken. The mogo is crispy and cut into bite-size chunks rather than the standard chip shape, though it's hard to eat with your fingers because of the sticky sauce.

I order off the Indian menu and large, well marinated chunks of chicken tikka pieces arrive. The food is tapas-like here and shows that the bar is king and the food complements it, rather than the other way round. I can see the North London inspiration here, and everyone seems to be happy, especially my friend who usually travels further afield for his pubs.

If your town's culinary and drinking scene needs livening up, like Caterham, then you should hope that an enterprising publican like Shukla takes a punt and opens up a desi pub.

Gladstone Arms

64 Lant Street, London SE1 1QN
T 020 7407 3529 · thegladpub.co.uk
Pub: Mon–Thu 12.00–23.00; Fri & Sat 12.00–24.00; Sun 12.00–23.00.
Kitchen: Mon–Sun 12.00–15.00, 17.30–22.00.

Borough is a key part of my desi pub journey. The Blue Eyed Maid on the High Street was the first ever British-Asian boozer I visited, about 15 years ago. It was run by a guy called Jay and wasn't the type of place you'd expect to feature in a guide to pubs. It was a dive bar that stayed opened till the early hours, a sticky-floored venue that featured raucous karaoke singing from the various waifs and strays who had wandered in because other bars had closed. Despite its dinginess, it was a safe place because Jay wouldn't tolerate any kind of abuse and employed a team of desi bouncers. He was one of the most empowered brown people I had then met and was always a friendly presence. Sadly, the pub stayed shuttered after the pandemic struck, and the last I heard of Jay he had moved back to his birth country. I am forever indebted to him.

Luckily, another desi pub that did survive is the Gladstone Arms (aka the Glad), which was reopened by brother-and-sister team Megha and Gaurav Khanna (and chef Abhinav Saxena, Meg's ex-husband who left a few years ago) in April 2017 after a CAMRA campaign successfully kept the pub open.

The Glad is a very different experience to the Maid. It's a small, cosy pub that offers comforting food and a relaxed drinking environment. Instead of karaoke, there's decent live music and excellent stand-up comedy. That's not to say that the pub isn't busy at weekends, it's just more welcoming to different types of drinker. Whereas the Maid was for young boozers, here young and old, rich and poor rub shoulders with each other.

As well as being sociable people, the Khannas are also heroes. Soon after they opened, the London Bridge terror attacks took place and they realised how important a community pub was to the area. They allowed the Glad to be a refuge for people fleeing the sickening scenes, offering free drinks and allowing strangers to charge their phones or to use the toilets.

Meg and Gaurav Khanna

Gaurav and Meg make you feel welcome and are such good conduits to conversation. On a first visit, they will introduce you to their gang and you'll soon become part of their wonderful world, which is a soothing balm when city life becomes isolating.

'We're like a local family,' says James Platt, who visits with his two Jack Russell dogs most weekdays. 'Which is unusual for a London pub. This is a totally non-judgemental place and everybody is welcome. So you get a lot of very diverse people coming in. [Meg and Gaurav] are interested in their customers. They like what [beers] they sell and they want to please the people who come in.'

The beers Platt mentions are sourced by Gaurav. He's the first desi publican to invest in craft – the Glad is particularly good for sours and smoked beers – and really knows how to run a good cellar. Gaurav shows

ndon Pride

that the desi pub tradition of selling macro lagers to go with decent food is outdated and he's keen to educate his customers.

There's also always one good cask selection on offer and pints of London Pride were served to a group of 30 CAMRA drinkers who arrived on a quiet Monday afternoon, much to their satisfaction. The feedback from drinkers is always overwhelmingly positive and shows the Glad has more than one market – anyone who loves beer and food will love this pub.

Platt is more than qualified to talk about diversity and how the pub has changed. In the 90s he used to come when it was a gay bar but was put off when it was taken over by publicans who ran it as a music venue. Other locals I speak to get the impression that non-music people who came just for a quiet drink were more tolerated than celebrated. Every regular I speak to you used the same phrase about the Khannas: 'We knew it would work as soon as we met them.'

Apart from the music, which includes Indian bands during Diwali and other celebrations, the other key facet the Khannas retained was the pies. Under the previous owners they were traditional Pieminister pies (think steak and kidney, chicken and mushroom), but now they are called 'Anglo-Indian' and include fillings such as chicken tikka masala, paneer makhani and goat keema.

Rachana Ramchand, who grew up in Wales and Sheffield, discovered the pub in 2018 and loves the cuisine and the Indian spirits, such as Old Monk. She tells me that usually this type of fusion food is a lot more expensive and it's rare to eat it in such a relaxed pub environment.

'When [my parents] entered a pub in the 1990s in Wales or Sheffield, they said they would look or feel different,' she says. 'I feel that difference too when I go back there. If the Glad was owned by a white person, it wouldn't be as close [to my heart] as it is.'

'When we opened the Glad five years ago, we had hardly any Indian customers,' says Meg. 'Then people started seeing the food, the spirits and Diwali events, and now 30–40% of our customers are Indian.'

The Indian-owned nature of the pub (the Khannas grew up in Zambia but are Punjabi in origin) is probably why it doesn't appear on many beer writers' lists when they talk about Borough. When (mostly white) beer writers recommend pubs in SE1 they will mention the Rake, the Lord Clyde and the Royal Oak, but rarely find space for the Glad, despite it being the finest modern iteration of a desi pub.

The Glad also highlights the male-dominated world of desi pubs: Meg is the only woman I've interviewed in this book who runs one. The reason for this lies in the fact that Punjabi drinking culture was traditionally very male and seen as a bastion of masculinity at the expense of women. Luckily, Meg and Gaurav had progressive parents who had no objections to them running a pub. (One landlord I speak to in the Midlands believes this will change in the future as Asian women feeling comfortable in desi pubs is a relatively recent development.)

'On my mum's side,' she says on a phone call while she's taking a well-earned holiday in India, 'it's pretty traditional but they've changed a lot.

There was a time when the men would drink on Fridays and they would close the doors and be on their own. The women weren't allowed to drink or even go into that room.

The only difference Meg can see with her family now is over the issue of restraint. 'It's not a culture where you get wasted in front of your family. In some parts of Britain people get really merry with their mum or dad, but it's not like that in our culture,' she says. 'Even if they came to London to visit the pub, there's still a line that we don't cross.'

The pub's proximity to London Bridge station means Meg can live in Dartford, while Gaurav stays at the Glad. Meg has told me how she gets funny looks when she goes to pubs there on her own. She's not sure if this is due to being a woman on her own or being brown.

'It's really important that Asian people feel pubs are safe places. I went to a pub once in the north and people were just looking at us. It's really important that you can go to a pub, play your own music, [eat] your own food, feel like you're part of the community and just make new friends. That's what pubs are about, right?'

Exactly. I took my young daughter for a Sunday roast at the Glad. She loves this dish, alongside mild chicken curries, but was a bit unsure about

Glad pies being made

Gladstone Arms

Chicken tikka pie

having a 'spicy' variation (like their hugely popular pies, the roasts are a fusion dish and have traditional trimmings with 'spicy' meats). The butter chicken 'supreme' roast is a thing of wonder, but my daughter particularly loves the railway lamb chops which come with roast potatoes that are crispy on the outside and nice and fluffy on the inside.

None of these dishes are as hot as ones I've tried at other desi pubs. That's because the meals were devised by Meg's ex-husband. The food has to be at this heat level because the fusion of Indian with 'British' pub grub wouldn't work otherwise. It's the prefect metaphor for how the Khannas have fused the best of Britain and the best of India. It's a true London and Punjabi success story.

Here they've managed to take our best pub traditions and combine them with desi hospitality to create a drinking experience that will make it your favourite local even if you live far away. Take Rachana Ramchand, for example, she travels from North London to come to the pub, and I know British-Indians who travel from Southall and Brighton for its unique experience.

No matter where you live, I urge you to follow suit and make the Glad your local.

African Queen

315–317 Wellington Road South, Hounslow TW4 5HL
T 020 8572 8903
aqbarandrestaurant.co.uk
Mon–Thu 15.00–24.00; Fri–Sun 12.00–24.00 (kitchen closes around 22.00).

Hounslow is a place I've grown to love after frequent visits to its desi pubs. Its proximity to Heathrow means it's similar to Southall with a rich Punjabi heritage (a total of 37% identify here as Asian) and has a strong, diverse community.

Nowadays, Hounslow is often maligned for being noisy as it's on the airport flightpath, but there are other parts of the capital where the noise pollution is just as bad. And if you're in a pub with a beer and grill on the go, a distant rumble won't be an issue.

Choosing which pub for this entry was difficult. I'm a big fan of the Black Horse (see photo right), for example, which mixes a community feel with Indian food and has a diversity of men and women of all ages and colour. It's the type of pub you would find in Smethwick (in fact, some of the regulars travel from here on the

Harry Mungali in the Black Horse, Hounslow (see p6)

coach heading to the Red Cow, p130), and is usually my go-to type of place.

But if, like me, you love looking for new experiences then the African Queen might be the place to visit, with its intriguing mix of great – even challenging – food in a humble setting. The building is the polar opposite of the recently redecorated Black Horse. It has a very basic, retro interior that feels like an old-fashioned curry house with a strange, blue-ish light, while the exterior is faded Mock Tudor that has seen much better days.

If this sounds disorientating, then you also have to come to terms with the misleading pub name – it was previously owned by a desi of Kenyan origin until it was bought eight years ago by a publican of Punjabi origin. Before all this it was a traditional boozer called the Plough.

It's a small-ish building, so the atmosphere can be a bit stilted on a quiet weekday (and it has a strong desi clientele, which also marks it as different to the Black Horse), but full marks to the woman working the bar who tried to inject some life into the place and was a jolly, friendly presence.

You might be wondering why I consider this to be one of the best desi pubs in London. The answer is that because the food is so good you forget the decor, vibe and blue gloam when you take your first bite. It's like a greatest hits of the food I've tasted writing this book, incorporating all the sage advice chefs and publicans have given when compiling Punjabi-inspired dishes – particularly Harry Khinda at the Crafty Indian (p168) who stated that Indian food doesn't necessarily have to be hot.

This is shown with the Punjabi chicken (off the bone, on the bone wasn't available) which is spicy with a garam masala kick, a smooth sauce and lots of ginger. The AQ wings, on the other hand, were really hot and came sizzling on a bed of onions, like a mini grill, while the fish pakora had a lovely batter ratio – perfect for drinks – and had a sprinkling of chaat masala.

It was so good that my companion, a brewer, started to praise the beer ('the lines are super clean'), and the atmosphere ('the place is homely like the food'). Which shows that this is the place to go when you want the food (and drink) to be the best part of your evening. No wonder there were so many people here dining solo.

It's not African. It's not glamorous. But it is nice to be here alone.

AQ wings

Scotsman

96 Scotts Road, Southall, Middlesex UB2 5DE
scotsmanpub.co.uk
T 020 8574 1506
Mon–Sat: 11.00–00.30; Sun: 12.00–23.30.

For many folk – brown and white alike – Southall can be a disorientating place. In its heyday it was a home from home for the South Asian diaspora, with an array of shops, market stalls and restaurants that were, to many British people, very exotic, and because it focused on the whole of Asia, it had a theme park feel. In fact, an Indian historian friend of mine found it 'inauthentic' when he visited because of the way in which a dated version of South Asia was being presented to him. In essence, though, this is desi culture.

It took me a while to understand it fully, and to appreciate its appeal, but I'm now a big fan of Southall, for these are some of London's most remarkable streets.

The key to the neighbourhood's success is that it includes Sikhs, Muslims, Hindus and Christians who are all from Punjab. The former is the biggest group, but everyone here lives relatively harmoniously. It might not be a utopia – it has social issues, like most parts of London – but when India, and particularly Punjab, fractured after partition in 1947 it was said that these groups couldn't live alongside each other. In this way, it's unlike most other Asian areas in the country.

Unlike, say, Brick Lane in East London, it's not built on one type of hospitality, like Bangladeshi curry houses, although there are plenty of decent restaurants here. Southall is more of a city within a city, and British Asians still flock here at night to enjoy the unique atmosphere, and to take advantage of the very reasonably priced goods and services. A friend, Saptarshi Ray, who used to work in Southall for a magazine, said, 'We used to joke that this place gets more and more like India every day. It's only a matter of time before you see a cow walking down the high street.'

Things have calmed down a bit from the heyday Ray mentions, when Southall used to be featured in Hindi films and broke into the UK

Shinda Mahal

mainstream after the movie *Bend it Like Beckham*. Glassy Junction, which was just by the train station (as mentioned in the introduction), was a beacon for a lot of desis and slotted in well with all this Southall mayhem.

Today, the Elizabeth Line has made this West London outpost seem less isolated, and one of the jewels in its crown is the Scotsman. Although not (always) a party pub like Glassy Junction, it does house some of the hardest drinking British-Asians I've met in this country; the type that tell stories about Southall gangs and the National Front that would shock you sober.

While the booze might be functional here, the food is out of this world. We're talking jumbo naans, huge chicken lollipops, and breathtaking chops, all lovingly created by landlord Shinda Mahal, who is steeped in heritage from the area because he used to work as a chef in – guess where? – Glassy Junction.

'Glassy was too busy!' he tells me. 'Not in the daytime in the week but on the weekends. People would go to weddings and the Gurdwara [and then come]. People would try to book or save seats, but we never allowed them.

'I learned the whole business from Glassy Junction when I first came to this country. I even accept rupees here like Glassy did.'

Yes, rupees. The idea behind this owes a lot to Southall's proximity to Heathrow. Someone would land from a flight from India and then their first port of call would be Glassy Junction – before they even had time to change their money into pounds. Nowadays, with contactless payments, it happens less and less, but it's interesting that the Scotsman still offers this slice of desi pub heritage.

The Scotsman had the same desi owners as Glassy Junction, and Mahal took over from them in 2008. He tells me that 15 years later he's made the place renowned for the jumbo naans, mixed grills and the chicken lollipops – which I thought at first were drumsticks but are, in fact, large wings. 'Every single table orders them!' he says.

It's a large pub, with sections that can be used for celebrations and private parties. This can be birthdays or weddings, where desis get together to toast their loved ones in a place that was previously hostile. Mahal admits things were very different in the Scotsman before it became a desi pub.

'Into the 80s,' he says about the pub before it was bought by the owners of Glassy Junction 'no Indians were allowed. Then they allowed us in [in the 90s] but only one side.'

What Mahal is describing is how the colour bar used to work. At first, all non-whites were banned from entering the pub, then it segregated its customers – probably because the racist owners needed the income and grudgingly served the wider community. It might seem hard to believe that

Jumbo naan

such segregation could exist in modern London, but this carried on until the mid 1990s.

Witnessing this prejudice first hand never dimmed Mahal's love for the area, which is now, thankfully, very diverse and inclusive.

'It's amazing,' he says. 'Totally different [to the rest of the country]. People know about [Southall] in India and all over England and that 80% of the community is Punjabi.'

He then tells me about a video of a World Cup cricket match that he posted on YouTube which shows the place heaving with people chanting 'India!' and sounding horns. It really is the spiritual successor to Glassy Junction. But if you think this would be intimidating, then think again. I've brought all different types of people here, particularly friends who haven't ever visited Southall before. Nick lives in New York and when he visited a few months ago, it took a lot of convincing to come here to watch an England football game (he normally sticks to the centre of London). When he stepped off the train, though, he was quite emotional as Southall reminded him of Queens, where his mother grew up. When I took him to the Scotsman he was impressed by the food – the quantity and quality – and the naan 'hanging from some kind of hook'.

'It's a special fusion place,' he told me on the way back. 'It was made all the more special by how normally all the patrons treated it. I can't believe they seemed to take it for granted.

'America is famous for being a melting pot but modern Britain just does the real thing without making a fuss about it.'

I do feel that the Scotsman is the best of London, but it's not a pub that ever features on any 'best of' lists, which shows how much places like Southall are ignored, despite their rich culture and excellent track record on diversity. It's also the first pub I felt truly safe in during the day when I visited it two years ago. I feel embarrassed at being 44 years old and having to explain this – but I've never felt like I could be truly comfortable in a pub where mine is the only non-white face. During the day pubs are more likely to have an older or more affluent clientele. Daytime drinking is a pursuit I enjoy, but I feel vulnerable doing it as I'm a brown outlier. Here, I don't feel that way, with numerous uncles at the bar accepting me for who I am.

I'm not sure they would be quite as accepting if I were a woman sitting on my own, especially if a match was on, though Megha Khanna from the Gladstone (p68) did visit here, and the nearby Prince of Wales, and wasn't put off by being in the minority.

I do feel that the Scotsman can claim to be one of the best pubs in London, however you wish to measure it, especially when you consider its torrid history. I do think it's time we made a fuss about it, because this is the real thing.

Chicken lollipops

South of England

The Drink Valley

Fleet Square, Swindon SN1 1RU
thedrinkvalley.com
Bar: *Tue 16.00–22.00; Wed–Sun 12.00–22.00.*
Kitchen: *Thu–Sat 12.00–21.00.*

The Drink Valley is the ultimate taproom in terms of beer, food and inclusion. It's also the place I recommend most if you want interesting cask beer made by a desi who is one of the best unknown brewers in the country.

All the cask lines (and most of the keg) are brewed by Dhiraj Pujari and the food is cooked by his wife, Deepali. The interior is light and airy, providing a more wholesome alternative to the various town centre bars (including a giant JD Wetherspoon opposite).

Dhiraj studied his Masters in brewing and distilling at Heriot-Watt, Edinburgh, in 2008, which was a big change for him. 'It was the first time I had left India,' he says. 'Yes, it was a big culture shock.'

Dhiraj worked in Leeds when he graduated, was offered a job at Purity but eventually ended up at Malborough-based Ramsbury brewery. 'When I started it was a 10-barrel brewery. Then they moved to 30 barrels and installed a distillery – so I was very important, production-wise.'

He worked there for nearly 10 years until 2020 when he decided to go it alone, a risky but nevertheless rational move for such a visionary character who can brew quality beers and who enjoys experimenting.

'My whole brewing career is in the UK so it's craft [focused] but I personally prefer keg due to the fizziness,' he tells me. 'Nowadays craft means hazy IPAs and DIPAs, but with us the biggest sellers are our real ales.'

These cask ales are excellent, and because of the way Dhiraj brews, they are just as 'crafty'. Yes, there are best bitters (which I adored), but there's also an IPA brewed with Simcoe hops (giving a nice grapefruit tone) called Go With The Flow.

'No recipe has been repeated, and since we've opened [in September 2020] we've done 52 brews.'

Deepali's most popular dish is railway chicken curry but there are plenty to choose from, especially on Thursdays when a curry and a drink costs £11.99. A popular Friday special is a beer and biryani for the same price.

The biggest thrill for me, though, is that, finally, I've discovered a place that serves great desi food with cask beer brewed by a British-Indian.

The Drink Valley

Easy Tiger @ The Hampton

57 Upper North Street, Brighton BN1 3FH · T 01273 731347
easytigerbrighton.com
Bar: *Mon–Thu 15.00–23.00; Fri–Sun 12.00–24.00.*
Kitchen: *Mon–Thu 17.00–21.00; Fri 12.00–15.00, 17.00–21.00;*
Sat 13.00–21.00; Sun 13.00–19.00.

The Bedfordshire town of Dunstable, where I grew up in the early 90s, wasn't at all racially diverse. I was the only non-white kid in my school, and when I started to frequent pubs when I was older I would be the only face of colour.

At the time, I hid my Asian culture – which wasn't difficult because my parents encouraged me to do so, wanting my sister and I to fit in. This meant I would tolerate local pub goers' racist views and prejudice and look to find common ground, sparking conversations about football rather than politics. Thankfully, I don't need to do this in a desi pub.

Areas that tend to have desi pubs are situated in Asian-majority enclaves such as Southall and West Bromwich, so it's probably unrealistic to expect a market town with poor transport links to have a desi pub culture when there are so few Asians.

So when I find a desi pub in a setting where there are few brown faces, I smile, because the younger me would have discovered this place with wide-eyed wonder. When I enter The Easy Tiger @ The Hampton in Brighton my first thought is how much a younger me would have enjoyed supping his first pint in such comforting surroundings.

The pub was the brainchild of Kanthi Thamma who is now in charge of nearby Palmito – a spice-driven small plates venue – and is a chef who is used to changing people's perceptions of what Indian food *should* be. But there are limits.

'If we serve anything apart from Indian food then people will stop coming,' he says about Easy Tiger, where his distinct dishes are now prepared by a chef he trained.

He believes that around 96% of his customers come to eat, which is surprising considering the range of craft beers on offer and the Hampton's

Kanthi Thamma

classic pub layout. But the food is a huge draw for good reason – it's all fresh ingredients and uniquely desi. Kanthi regularly travels to Kerala in South India, finding new dishes to add to his menu. He also sources spices from there and tries to have everything organic unless it means raising his prices above pub food fare.

This is as close as you can get to fine dining in a pub setting without having to blow your budget. And it's all put together by a chef who has worked in Michelin-starred restaurants around the world with a philosophy that Indian food should be vibrant, evolving, and a mixture of modern and 'desi'.

'I was looking for a pub,' says Kanthi. 'I always wanted to do Indian food in a pub because it works. Everyone talks about beer and Indian food – it's a given. I never thought it would be so popular!'

This might seem like a modern story, but the leitmotif of desi pub regeneration is in Easy Tiger's DNA. Before Kanthi got together with the team behind Brighton's Pond and Star and Garter, the Hampton was, in his words, 'run down, falling apart. No one went there'. Now it's flourishing, and packed out on evenings and weekends.

When I visited nearly a year ago I was still coming to terms with how the book should take shape and what its main themes should be. When I asked

Kanthi what he thought the term desi was, I was a bit taken aback by his answer: 'Desi is a feeling rather than an identity,' he replied.

This perfectly encapsulated the Indian diaspora's relationship with the word desi. When used with pubs it can be interpreted in so many ways, and it's fitting that the most southern entry in this book informed how flexible my approach was to 'desi-ness'. Was it used to describe people who drink in the pub? The food served? Or the way the landlord and customers expressed their culture? All three of these definitions are common.

The other theme is boundaries – those of India and Britain – because 'desi' can be about preserving the feelings British-Indians had when they or their descendants left India for the UK. Which is ironic because the name Easy Tiger is itself about boundaries. Kanthi was freestyling names for the pub with his business partners and one of them went a bit too far, so he had to say 'easy, tiger!'

It's a great name, as you'll discover when you try the food, because it's so aggressively boundary-less when it comes to the dishes. This is food that can be eaten any way you like with your beers: snacking alone after a swim in the sea (as I did), sharing with mates, or dining with a date – are all possible.

And this shows what a good desi pub does best: allowing the customer to use it in as many ways as possible.

Easy Tiger @ The Hampton

Fishponds Tap

693 Fishponds Road, Bristol BS16 3UH
T 0117 987 2570 · fishpondstap.co.uk
Pub: Mon–Thu 12.00–23.00; Fri & Sat 12.00–24.00; Sun 12.00–23.00.
Kitchen: Mon–Thu 12.00–22.00; Fri & Sat 12.00–23.00; Sun 12.00–22.00.

Abhi Paudel has taken on a huge project by opening a desi pub. Bristol is not curry-literate, unlike other Britain's other major urban centres. The locals I speak to who have lived in other parts of the country admit that the few curry houses in the city are fairly standard and far behind those you'll find in places like London, Leeds or the Midlands. And way behind the types I've mentioned elsewhere in this book.

Most of Paudel's customers in the Fishponds area of Bristol, therefore, aren't yet ready for the sort of dishes I've listed extensively – they think curries should be low-cost fast food. But this is an opportunity for the desi landlord. As locals realise he's selling high quality fare, something a world away from the nearby Wetherspoons, he'll soon have a monopoly of this market.

Paudel is Nepalese and his food will be familiar to those who have visited the Aroma Lounge in Wembley (he's the uncle of the landlord there, see p32). As well as trying to convert residents to 'exotic' Indian dishes, he also serves momos, delicious Nepalese dumplings, and as I take photos of these mouth-size pockets of joy, the locals start to stare and point, realizing there might be more to this pub's food than the burgers they've ordered without giving too much thought to it.

Paudel's chef, Dinesh, has worked with Michelin-starred Indian chef Atul Kochhar at Vaasu in Marlow, Buckinghamshire.

'There are good restaurants in Bristol,' Paudel says. 'But when it comes to Indian restaurants, I prefer my food. And the Google reviews show that. The only bad one I got someone was saying my TV was too big!

'No one was given the choice before [of high-quality food] and if I was to offer it, people would want it. Food is the lifeline of the pub.'

And this lifeline was supplied by Paudel, who invested hugely in the Fishponds, refurbishing what was becoming a shabby and dilapidated

Fishponds Tap

Abhi Paudel

interior. The £500,000 spent means there's now a lavish function room and large beer garden. A lot of his customers, though, are surprised to find a brown face in charge of such a large pub, even though he has a degree in hospitality and learned his trade in a desi pub in north London for 12 years.

'A customer once looked at me and asked "why would you run a pub?"' he tells me. 'My answer is "this is what I know". I'm Asian. I'm a desi. I'm from Nepal. I've been in the hospitality industry for a long time and have run bars and pubs before.'

Before I started visiting the many desi pubs around the country, I had this notion that the food served was great but often lacked 'home' flavours, that it was, in some way, inauthentic compared to family meals. This is something that Paudel, with his many years of experience and love of food, is keen to explain.

'The chutney,' he says, 'makes all the difference in the momos. My chef [Kochhar] is Nepalese and has his own secrets, but certain dishes, like the chutneys, are cooked by my wife because they can be home cooked.

'My wife is a brilliant cook. I can't ask this chef to make it – you need someone like my wife – they have only learned how to cook in restaurants.'

This wonderful mixture of home-cooked and restaurant food means you can have the best of both worlds – lovely sauces, thick curries and amazing

Fishponds Tap

Fishponds Tap

Momos at Fishponds Tap

naans. No one can recreate these restaurant-style naans at home. I loved the Himalayan Lamb Chops – subtly spiced with a deep marinade – and the Chili Paneer, smoky and cooked in a true 'home-made' sauce, which came before the mains.

Like the Aroma Lounge, you can find yourself just ordering from the starters, but Paudel doesn't miss a trick with the mains, and here you get a set meal – with a curry, rice and naan served for around £13–14. It does make the food less communal, however. It's a perfect self-contained meal and easy to order for customers who may not be sure of how these type of curries should work.

The Fishponds may be an unlikely desi destination, but it's slowly changing a city's attitude to Indian food.

The most remarkable thing about this part of Bristol is that even though it doesn't have a large South Asian community, opposite Paudel is another desi pub run by Sam Merchant called the **Railway Tavern**. Although this does seem like a natural desi food destination – it serves great cask beer and holds live music gigs – it does offer more humble fare. 'We do home-made curries,' Merchant says. 'Home-made from scratch. I make them.'

Ivy Inn

Arrow Lane, North Littleton, Evesham WR11 8EF
theivyinn.co.uk
Pub: Mon–Thu 16.00–22.00; Fri 16.00–23.00; Sat 12.00–23.00; Sun 12.00–22.00.
Kitchen: Mon–Sat 17.00–21.00; Sun 12.00–17.00.

When I show my friends photos of desi pubs, they're always keen to see the curries, the kitchens and the smiling landlords. They're never really interested in pub exteriors, which could be because the businesses tend to appear in locations that are sometimes unremarkable to the naked eye, though I think they always add a flavour of India to a drab high street.

But if I told you there was a country desi pub on the edge of the Cotswolds, you'd want to see the building first. I also imagine that you'd want to know how an establishment like the Ivy Inn can claim to be a desi pub when it has a mainly white customer base and only serves Indian food a couple of days a week.

The answer is landlord Kyle Mahli, son of Bera at the Red Cow (p130). Despite being in his early 20s, he is steeped in the history of desi pubs and realises that the way Punjabi culture can reach new areas is for pubs like this to open. It means children of first-generation desi landlords, like Mahli, have to move out of diverse areas like Smethwick and embrace rural life.

This might seem straightforward, but many people of colour, as in my case, prefer to stick to certain towns and cities. We enjoy the scenery, fresh air, and space, but have suffered rural racism, ranging from micro-aggressions

(being ignored, for example) to outright hostility (I have been called a 'Paki' throughout the years when I've ventured out of metropolitan areas).

I would like to live in the countryside one day, and what gives me hope is seeing someone like Mahli forge a life for himself here. He is very proud of where he grew up – he recalls his dad telling him when he was 12 about Malcolm X visiting Smethwick – but the lure of something different took hold.

'I wanted to get away from [the] Birmingham [area],' Mahli says. 'I wanted to get away from the busier lifestyle, take a step back and see what the quieter life is like.'

Mahli is one of the most resilient youngsters I've met. His life was spent in pubs, following his dad around and pouring pints when he was just eight years old. His love of the pub trade earned him the nickname 'Mini Bera', and he has the same enthusiasm as his father for explaining the philosophy behind desi pubs.

'My dad taught me that hard work was the main thing,' he says. 'My dad was in the pub every single day and I was in the pub every single day. We weren't on holiday: we had to work to live. I get a lot of confidence from my dad just from being with him and he taught me how deal with people in pubs and how to be sociable.

'Every day after school I'd be in the pub. If we did mobile bars at weddings, then I'd be there. I never spent a day at home I was always out with my dad.'

The usual story of taking over a pub that needed a huge facelift doesn't apply here as the building had a warm, comfortable bar and a Tudor-style, beamed lounge area. But that doesn't mean the business didn't need regeneration. It was trying to be a high-end restaurant, which didn't really work.

Kyle Mahli

Ivy Inn

'The previous customers,' says Mahli, 'told me they didn't feel comfortable coming in their workwear or just coming in for a drink. They said that the people who ordered food would always be more important than the drinkers.

'The first thing I wanted to change was that the pub wasn't mine. It was the villagers. Come after work with your high-viz [jacket] and muddy boots. Bring your dogs in. Everybody is welcome.'

In many ways this egalitarian approach is synonymous with all desi pubs. A desi may take over a pub and put their cultural imprint on it through food, drinks or events, but, ultimately, they want the pub to be cherished by all of the community. And Mahli is someone who is comfortable with different types of people, even if he is an outlier.

At the Red Fort, the club Bera ran before the Red Cow, the clientele included large groups from various communities. This also gave him the courage to own a pub with a customer base that is from a different background to his own.

'At one point,' he says, 'I'd be sat with a load of Irishmen back from work. Then a bunch of Jamaican lads, or old Indians, young Indians. There was every different culture. [It taught me] a pub is for everybody and there should never be any discrimination. When you come to a pub, everybody should be on an equal footing.'

The Ivy Inn

The Ivy Inn 'sizzler' with a pint of Purity UBU

The pub's food is standard fare, apart from a couple of days a week. I advise checking their website if you're after a mixed grill, though they're not called 'mixed grills' here because Mahli's customers, he admits, associate the name with the type of meat feast you'd find in a Harvester chain pub. Instead, they're called 'sizzlers', which is often what a mixed grill is called on menus in India.

'In every sense of the word,' Mahli says. 'It's exactly the same as a [desi pub] mixed grill. It's based on the Red Cow's mixed grill, and even though I am biased, I've never been anywhere and had a better mixed grill.'

The default curry setting is mild but can be spiced up depending on the customer's needs. There's even a create your own curry part to the menu, ideal if you're a mixed group of people or a family.

When I speak to Mahli he's looking to expand the kitchen. Traditional pubs tend to have smaller kitchens which can't fit multiple tandoors and hobs that desi pubs require. He employs just two chefs, a Nepalese head chef and a sous chef, who is keen to hear me talk about the other chefs I've met on my travels.

All that's left now is to ask Mahli about desi-ness and how he views the concept. 'With English people,' he concludes, 'everybody's separate. Once you become a certain age you go your own way and become very independent. Whereas with South Asians it's very family based – once you get married, once you have kids, you all kind to stay together.

'And I think that expands to the community, to friends, and the people you go to the pub with. I've got a very desi set of morals: do your best, never hurt anybody, try to help everyone and have fun.'

You can see now why Mahli – and other desis – make such good landlords.

The Runner

Wootton Bassett Road, Swindon SN1 4NQ
runninghorsepub.co.uk
Pub: *Sun–Thu 12.00–22.00; Fri–Sat 12.00–23.00.*
Kitchen: *Mon–Thu 12.00–15.00 & 17.00–21.00; Fri–Sat 12.00–22.00;*
   Sun 12.00–21.00.

Abhi Paudel is an empire builder. I interviewed him at his first pub, the Fishponds Tap (p85) about a year ago. Then the publican described a certain nervousness about opening up a desi pub in an area – Bristol – that wasn't exactly au fait with Indian food.

He needn't have worried. Since we last spoke, in 2022, the Fishponds has become a huge success, and he has opened another two pubs: the White Harte, in the affluent suburb of Warmley, and this one, The Runner, in Swindon. And though the former is a big success, he's most proud of the latter.

You can see why: it's a beautiful country pub tied to a family brewery that serves wonderful cask beer. In fact, Swindon has an old-fashioned, soothing relationship with Arkell's, reminding me of those grand pub estates of well-run plush pubs encasing a town and creating a hospitality microclimate of fine local beers served expertly to a knowledgeable crowd.

For Arkell's to include a desi pub in their portfolio is a big deal. 'I can proudly say,' Paudel tells me, 'There are no other pubs like this. Arkell's used to run the pub themselves and we're the first ever tenant of this pub.'

When the pub came on the open market, Paudel wasn't convinced Arkell's would go into partnership with him, not only because he lived in Bristol but also because the old building had never been used to cook meals on an industrial scale (as is often necessary in desi pubs). But on the first meeting, the brewer offered the Runner to him straight away, knowing he would make a success of it.

Paudel and his business partner (and friend), Bisnukumar Gurung, were given the keys in February, 2023 and shut the pub for a week for a small refurbishment.

'All the Arkell's pubs have a very basic kitchen,' Paudel says. 'Some sandwiches. Some burgers maybe. A few weeks after we opened we started the

Bisnukumar Gurung

Arkell's
Wiltshire Gold

Tandoori wings

food, and when I visited the kitchen I got scared. It was so smoky. The type of food we do – the grill, the spices – there was a lot of fumes. We installed a new canopy extractor system.'

The kitchen has been the only change to the Runner and it's still deeply embedded in the community and valued by locals. Every year there's a charity duck race, for example, when 15,000 toy ducks are raced on the stream that runs through the beer garden, attracting 400–500 people on a bank holiday.

But this isn't two desis serving a wholly white clientele. 'There's a Nepalese community,' says Nepal-born Paudel. 'And the other community we attract is the Goan one. But the locals were so pleased that we took over because we were taking the pub somewhere different – the pub had no consistency with food, service and drinks.

'It used to shut at 5pm on a Sunday. They didn't have the passion. You need to have the passion.'

The food offering is the same as at the Bristol pub (two menus – Nepalese-Indian and traditional) but a few additions have been made since I visited. I try the tandoori wings, which are pleasant but not fiery because the heat levels are tailored for a traditional audience. I even tried a paneer pizza, which was a worthy bucket-list experiment.

The best day to visit, though, would be Sunday when roasts are cooked desi-style with marinated spicy meats served with the usual British trimmings. 'It's a roast with a bit of a twist,' adds Gurung. 'Tandoori chicken with gravy. The beef is the same (unspiced) but the chicken is the most popular roast.'

The whole concept of a desi pub is mirrored by this dish because that's what a British–Indian pub offers: tradition with a twist.

V's Punjabi Grill at the Canal Tavern

Canal Road, Gravesend, Kent DA12 2RS
T 01474 247737 · vspunjabigrill.co.uk
Pub: Mon–Sat 12.00–22.00; Sun 11.00–21.00.
Kitchen: Mon–Thu & Sun 12.00–14.00, 17.00–21.00; Sat 12.00–14.00, 17.00–22.00.

When I worked at a daily financial newspaper 15 years ago I had to wade through a lot of language that I found impenetrable. But one useful term I still remember today was 'bellwether'. It's something that signifies that the economy was booming or busting. In those more carefree days, it tended to be sales of luxury watches, giant restaurant tips or orders for new taxi carriages.

Writing this book, I often considered 'bellwethers' that would alert me to an area that could contain a desi pub when I was looking at regions outside of London and Birmingham that readers could visit. Unfortunately, there are no hard and fast rules, and somewhere with a high Sikh population, a Gurdwara, and a taste for Indian food doesn't necessarily lead to a desi pub culture. Liverpool is the prime example of this. A Liverpudlian Sikh friend – who loves desi pubs – tells me that the city's Sikh community tends to socialise around the temple and that it's not a place you will see many brown-skinned drinkers.

Unlike Liverpool, though, a lot of places that have those three bellwethers of Sikhs, temples and Indian food tend to have at least one desi pub, and Gravesend proves this rule of three: 8% Sikh population according to the 2021 census, a beautiful Gurdwara, a large number of curry houses.

Bera Mahli, from the Red Cow (p130) in Smethwick, went to school here when he arrived decades ago, and encountered lot of racism. In 2022, though, things are different, according to the guys who run V's Punjabi Bar and Grill. They couldn't be more intertwined in the community. In fact, a strong community identity is perhaps one of the best bellwethers as to whether an area will have a desi pub.

And this pub is more neighbourly than most, especially as it doubles as a vaccination clinic. The owner, Raj Choprav, is a pharmacist who realised the town he grew up in did not have enough capacity for Covid jabs.

This led to national headlines of 'kebabs and jabs', and I was amused to see a queue of masked pensioners waiting in what looked like a surgery queue while smoking mixed grills were whisked past them by busy waiters.

'I spoke to my MP,' says Choprav, whose dad did get very ill with Covid when the first wave struck. 'And we've got nice marquee out there. So I thought "why not give something back to the community?"'

Choprav is able to do this vital medical work because he hired Clifford Rodrigues to manage the pub. Rodrigues is the co-landlord, allowing Choprav to be the behind-the-scenes businessman. It's a partnership that relies on trust and it clearly works. The pub had a lovely friendly atmosphere when I visited in autumn.

'His CV said he managed Eye Candy in Dubai,' Choprav says. 'My wife and I had just visited there on honeymoon – it had nice ambience, nice cocktails. I thought this must be fate and I hired him on the spot.'

It was a wise move because Rodrigues really knows how to make a desi pub work by ensuring that even when it's packed the drinks flow quickly and regulars are treated royally. He visited the pub before it became V's Punjabi Bar and Grill and was amazed that it was empty during a big football match, with owners who didn't put customers first.

'[The then landlord] said "guys we're closing. Drink up!"' Rodrigues tells me. 'It was during a big football match! We had to walk to another pub and when we came back next week he did the same thing. I asked him if he needed help running the place.

'He said, "I'm not investing. This place is being taken over." I gave him my CV [to give to Choprav].'

Before the duo took over, the pub had fallen into disrepair, and like many desi landlords they set about renovating the place so it could serve the quality food that sets it apart from anything else on offer in Gravesend. The kitchen is now modern and very large, in fact about four times the size of the one used by the previous landlord (which would have been a fire hazard if anyone attempted to work a tandoor or make a smoking mixed grill).

But the kitchen was the least of the problems. 'We moved a cupboard downstairs in the cellar,' Choprav says. 'And there was standing water that had been there for years. There were rats!'

Nowadays, luxury is the key to the pub's success. The food is amazing, the atmosphere is great and the bar is bright and welcoming. The mixed grill I have is spiced perfectly and there's a lovely view of the nearby canal. The pub's clientele is surprisingly diverse – not just in terms of race – but in age and gender.

When there's a football match on, the pub sells out weeks in advance – they didn't even need to advertise that they were showing games when the last major tournament was being played. But this isn't just a bar full of desis

V's Punjabi Grill

with Liverpool and Man United tops cheering their teams on while they eat mixed grills.

'It's a real mix,' Rodrigues says. 'A lot of English people who come down for the first time are very impressed with the food. They say, "this is my favourite Indian," and I say, "excuse me. It's not Indian. It's Punjabi."

'We wanted it to be upmarket,' Choprav continues. 'As well as being more homestyle food. Our chefs have originated from Punjab. We don't scrimp on costs when it comes to the quality of ingredients and the time the chefs put into cooking it. The food speaks for itself, and we have so many returning customers.'

I can see why. The mixed grill they served me had some of the best chicken wings I've ever tasted, with a marinade that was soaked deep into the meat. I knew it would be good, though, as the best bellwether for a great desi pub is the warm welcome you receive when you enter.

Mixed grill

The Midlands

Grove

279 Grove Lane, Birmingham
T 0121 554 3120
facebook.com/grovepub
Mon–Sun 11.00–23.00.

Handsworth, like Smethwick, was a former battleground of prejudice that has become a shining example of how Britain can navigate a past beset by racism. The nearby Handsworth Horticultural Institute was infamous for only allowing white members to join, right up to its closure, and pubs were hostile places for Asians and Black members of the local community. Then the Grove was opened by Piara Singh, 71, who first set up this large community pub in 1995 to serve British-Indians working in the foundries.

When I arrive at the pub early on a Saturday morning, I'm allowed inside to wait (in the dark) for Singh who isn't expecting me (communication is often difficult with proprietors of busy, established pubs, and often I have to turn up unannounced hoping I haven't wasted a journey).

Singh arrives, the lights are turned on, and the show begins. He explains how much this area has changed, as well as subtly hinting at the part he played in creating a more inclusive community.

Singh is Birmingham's longest-running pub licensee; he started pulling pints in 1976 at a pub called the Wonder Vaults in Winston Green. He arrived in the country when he was just aged 15, sent here with members of his elder family while his dad still lived in Kenya. The upheaval was difficult to adjust to, especially because Handsworth in the late 1960s was a hostile place for anyone arriving from outside.

'There were not many Asian people in school,' Singh says. 'It was tough – they would kick our asses.' Sport gave him a community and he played Kabaddi as part of a Gurdwara team with Bera at the Red Cow (see p130), driving around the country in a white van.

Singh is living and breathing social history and remembers going to pubs when British-Indian foundry workers would take their lunch breaks and buy two pints of Ansells Mild 3.2% for half a crown. Today the pub

still has M&B Mild on for its older Asian customers, but back
in the day it was Ansells Mild and Bitter, Guinness and Skol.

'When we opened,' Singh says. 'Asian people would come to
us from all around. We had some trouble from [white people]
but we calmed them down.'

In those times desi pubs were famous for playing Indian
records from a jukebox, but food wasn't served. In fact, Singh
confirms that the Vine (p152) was the first in the area to serve food
when an outdoor grill was built. In those days mild would be so
popular that three or four 36-gallon barrels would be sold a week
– no surprise when you consider how hot the foundries were.

'Our people work hard,' Singh says. '[The foundries] had no fans.
No windows. Nothing. I worked there for three months after school and
my hands were burned. It was too hard for me because I hadn't worked
in India [like the other workers].'

The Grove was much smaller then, with a beer garden, which was
extended into to create the huge space I'm confronted with today. The idea
of a wet pub only serving Punjabi men is a far cry from today where a huge
number of mixed grills are ordered as sharing platters to a mixed crowd of
men, women, white, black and brown. It's also not tied to one football club;
an equal number of Aston Villa and West Bromwich Albion fans visit before
and after their games. Harmony is the watchword of the modern Grove.

The refurb a few years ago really changed the pub, especially for women
and children. Nina Robinson grew up in the area in a Punjabi family and her
father, who worked in the local foundry, would drink with other men at the

Singh's nearby Manor Grove, built on the site
of the Handsworth Horticultural Institute

Grove

Piara Singh

weekend. She never felt particularly welcome in the Grove in the past but now the atmosphere has radically changed.

'It became more acceptable for women to go there,' she says. 'And the real turning point was when I thought it was OK for my kids to come to this pub on a Saturday night. The fact that I felt like I could do that in a really busy desi pub was a watershed moment.'

Robinson's favourite dish is the fish pakora, which I tried during my visit. They were excellent, as were the tandoori wings (a friend of mine who is a food video blogger and photographer says the Grove serves the best desi pub grub).

It's good news for Singh who is soon to retire and is leaving the pub in the more than capable hands of his son Manjeet, with his other sons, Gurjit, Amankaur and Sukhwinder helping. It won't be a huge change, though, as Singh also explains that a surprisingly large number of staff members have stuck with him, including Sandra who has been working the bar for more than 25 years.

'My son [Manjeet] was 17 or 18 years old when he pulled his first pint,' says Singh. 'I put him in the business first. I'm retiring soon but I'll always come back here. When I bought it it was so small and I worked very hard. Now electricity [bills] keep going up but we're doing ok because we have so many regulars and a good location.'

As the pub starts to fill with people wanting food, drinks, and to watch football and horse racing on the TVs, Singh reveals how he has stamped his mark on the wider community outside the pub.

Grove

A short-ish walk from the Grove is where the Handsworth Horticultural Institute once stood, a bastion of white supremacy, which steadfastly refused membership to Asians or Blacks. So it's fitting that Singh bought the place in 2014, sunk a fortune into it, and now uses it to host Indian celebrations. It's now called the Manor Grove and I'm taken aback by its size and splendour, and its well-drilled kitchen.

For British-Indians such as Robinson, these post-racism venues brought her family closer and have a huge cultural significance, especially for women – Singh's daughter-in-law, Sukhwinder, runs the Manor Grove. Robinson tells me that her parents recently celebrated their 50th wedding anniversary in a similar kind of place which, like visiting the Grove with her kids on a Saturday night, was another watershed moment.

'This shows a change in Indian family life in Britain,' she says. 'In the past the only Indian functions you were weddings, and this was the only time families would get together. Now we have other celebrations.'

Robinson feels this has been important in helping family members have closer relationships with each other, especially for fathers who could be more emotionally distant. Just the fact that her parents saw her being more affectionate to her own children made a huge difference.

'This level of affection allowed us to have these celebrations,' she says. 'I've done research into Punjabi ancestry, and villagers never used to celebrate themselves or have these kinds of relationships with each other.

'The fact that women are now in these spaces means they can organise things in a different way that's not centred around the Gurdwara and religion.'

For Singh it shows how much life has changed since his tenure at the Grove and the huge part he's played in making pubs turn from safe havens for British-Asians to inclusive environments for all.

Grove

Indian Brewery Snowhill

Arch 15–16 Livery Street, Birmingham B3 1EU
T 0121 296 9000
indianbrewery.com
Mon–Thu 12.00–21.00; Fri & Sat 12.00–22.00; Sun 12.00–20.00.

I noticed a curious trend when I was putting this book together: a stranger online with little or no desi pub experience would tell me unprompted what a desi pub was or wasn't.

Desi pubs aren't a phenomenon in Leeds, Manchester or Liverpool. These three large northern cities have a demand for spicy food washed down with beers, but have no history of British-Indians opening up pubs (with a few notable exceptions, see North of England & Scotland chapter.

The Indian street food firm Bundobust has, to a certain extent, plugged this gap by offering quality beers with vegan and vegetarian food in a relaxed dining environment. Some of their dishes are truly unique and their beers – particularly the Desi Mild (top marks for popularising the word 'desi') and Chai Porter – are always reliably brilliant. Their businesses also occupy vibrant, airy metropolitan spaces that can simultaneously feel intimate and communal.

It's this northern mini-chain that a lot of (white) people claim to be a desi pub, but even the founders of the business would blanch at the suggestion that they run desi pubs. That's not to say they don't like them; in fact, the opposite is true. They even held their Christmas party in the Keg & Grill (p108) and Soho Tavern (p116) in Birmingham.

The reason I don't think Bundobust fits my criteria for this book is because, when I've visited, I haven't seen many empowered British-Asians, and the waiting staff have been mainly white. Like I said, the food and dining experience they offer is great, while introducing their take on Indian dishes to a wider audience is refreshing, but they aren't the genuine, family-run desi business that you would find in the West Midlands or London.

The Indian Brewery Company, located in Snow Hill in Birmingham, by the train station, has claims to be exactly this kind of business.

With two brothers, Jaspal and Jay Purewal, brewing the beers, and their father in the kitchen, it really is the kind of space I relished visiting. The building in the railway arches looks functional (maybe even shop-like) from the outside but inside it's a light, vibrant space with excellent Indian-style decor.

The beer offering was huge and curated perfectly to fit the food that was being offered. On my visit I had a Birmingham Lager, which was mildly floral on the nose with spots of herbal scents, possibly tones of elderflower, and despite this sweetness it was subtle, citrusy, with a flavour that somehow lay in between lemon and lime. The Czech Saaz hops gave this pilsner-style, unfiltered beer a lovely depth.

I also highly recommend the Creamy Stout, which felt a lot stronger than its 4.2% ABV, with a coffee-like aroma, and the Peacock Lager, which was more Germanic than the Birmingham one, with a crisp mouthfeel and a prominent hoppy bitterness. It was great to get my notepad out and write down all the different flavours and how they paired with what was being served from the kitchen. This hasn't happened often enough.

The Birmingham Lager was the perfect drink to have with seafood and it paired wonderfully with my Indian Fish and Chips (spiced batter, served with masala chips). The dishes here are radical updates on what a desi pub could serve, paired with regional favourites.

Indian Brewery Snowhill

Silky sauce fries

So, as mentioned when I visited the near-ish Soho Tavern, chips are an important side dish, to be taken seriously in the Midlands. Here I have a choice of Masala fries, vegan mayo fries, curry sauce fries, saucy chili fries, keema fries and silky sauce fries.

I ordered the latter, which are a very modern update of curry sauce and chips (confusingly for writing this, the Indian Fish and Chips came with a more familiar style of Chip Shop curry sauce – fruity and thick, but not fatty). The silky sauce fries were very much like having a butter chicken sauce with chips. They were a very strong-tasting dish, which went indulgently well with the stout. The chips were very crispy – actually, I'd say they were perfectly cooked – and I would highly recommend having them as a side to any of the dishes on offer.

This food and beer, like Bundobust, moves away from the kind of offering desi pub customers can expect, and really is uncharted territory for a lot of people. When I visit there are no non-white customers, apart from myself and my Indian friend who is accompanying me. When I speak to Jaspal, he admits that a lot of people who frequent desi pubs find this approach too radical and are almost scared of trying something new.

That's not to say there aren't desi customers, they're just in the minority, and my friend Nina who lives in the area, swears by the fish faat naan, which is fried cod pieces, rocket salad, cucumber, and red onions topped with a sweet chili sauce. These are giant wraps and may be off-putting to some because of the cost (the fish faat naan is £14) when compared to a tikka roll, which usually is sold for half the price.

It's silly to compare the two, though, as this is an indulgent, multi-layered meal with many ingredients. This is excellent food at reasonable prices,

especially if you compare it to equivalent mid-range food and drink offerings, but here lies the paradox. This kind of setting suits people who are craft literate, whereas a lot of people who frequent desi pubs don't feel comfortable in this kind of setting.

Yes, it's a cultural thing, but it's also an issue with craft, or anything pitched as 'craft', as it tends to exclude people of colour by offering very little representation. I've been to the best craft bars, the best craft beer shows and the best craft taprooms: the beer is great, but even in diverse metropolitan areas, I'm the only person of colour. This is obviously a systemic issue, and it would help if more brewers were from different backgrounds. This is where the Purewals are trailblazers.

As they work out the best format for their business – they recently closed a satellite branch in Walsall and a brewery taproom – desi pub-goers should realise that they're doing something different while producing an offering that is still aimed at them. It might take a bit of courage for some to visit, but I urge you to take the plunge as it could be the future of the desi pub. In fact, I look forward to people recommending it back to me.

Keg & Grill

Unit 1, 20 Suffolk Street, Queensway, Birmingham B1 1LW
T 0121 632 6231
thekegandgrill.co.uk
Mon–Thu 16.00–22.00; Fri & Sat 14.00–22.30; Sun 14.00–21.00.

I hope after reading the numerous entries in this book that you'll understand how the desi pub is a very different beast to an Indian restaurant. The typical curry house – which was much more popular when I was growing up in the 80s and 90s – was usually run by Bangladeshis and aimed at a post-pub crowd.

The conditions were tough for these British–Asian frontline workers as racism was rife, drunkenness was common and there was little solidarity between restaurateurs, leading to low margins.

It's also true that the food was variable in quality and not really aimed at desis, who would have struggled to recognise some of the curries – I definitely didn't grow up eating vindaloo, although adding vinegar to curries as an ingredient can be tasty (hence the name). There was definitely a gap in the market for the diaspora to eat grills and spicy dishes.

When the first establishments designed for British-Asians were set up they either had to open as wet pubs or had to have a membership scheme in order to serve food. This was especially the case in London, as the Century Club (p62) and Regency (p44) demonstrate. As Peter Patel, founder of the Century, told me, 'Indians like to eat when they drink,' inferring that having a session of beer and then eating a curry was a pastime for white Brits.

There's one problem with Patel's theory: rice. Boiled grains, such as basmati or pilau, don't always lend themselves to simultaneous alcohol consumption, which, I think, is one of the many reasons why mixed grills are so popular with pub goers. So why not, on occasion, use a desi pub like an after-session curry house, particularly if it's sited near a boozer that doesn't do food?

This is the relationship the Craven Arms has with the Keg & Grill in central Birmingham. When a customer at the former wants food – apart from cobs (rolls) – they send them to the latter. This is done in reverse

Gee Bansal

when someone wants a large selection of fine real ales. The Craven is a Black Country ales pub, and though the Keg & Grill also kept some good cask when I visited (confusingly 'keg' is a word often used in India to mean 'glass', I'm told during my visit) it's not on the scale of its neighbour.

I can see why customers from the Craven are sent to the Keg & Grill as the food is exceptional, particularly if you want something a bit different from a mixed grill. On my visit, custodian Gurmit (Gee) Bansal said vegetarian food was very popular, so I tried a veggie grill. Out with the fish pakoras, shish kebabs and wings, in with flattened bhajis, soya tikka, sizzling samosas and spicy mushrooms cooked on the tandoor.

'You have to adapt to everyone's tastes,' Bansal says. 'It can't just be meat, meat, meat. The veggie platter is very popular. Not everyone caters for vegetarians but if you look at our reviews [online] they speak for themselves.'

The food appears simple but is revolutionary, especially if you're not a meat eater, or someone who loves desi pubs but wants to moderate their diet (like me). This tweak to a traditional Punjabi-inspired menu is somewhat surprising as Bansal grew up around Smethwick and his first taste of a desi pub was at the Red Cow (p130) in the late 1980s, before Bera Mahli took it over.

'They had a BBQ outside,' he says. 'They had lamb steaks, pork steaks and tandoori chicken legs. Every Friday we used to go there when my dad wanted some steaks – maybe have a glass while we're waiting for it.'

Bansal is steeped in desi pub culture and thinks the key to their success is that they offer everything in one place. No wonder hungry customers at the Craven get sent here. 'Before you would go for drinks and then go to a restaurant. But now you don't have to: you have your TV, your sports. You can be comfortable, relaxed and you have families coming in. In other pubs you sometimes get only one type of group coming in. But here it's a family environment.'

Bansal ran two pubs before the Keg & Grill – a wet bar followed by the Quinton Bar & Grill in the suburbs. But this boozer is in the heart of the city and has a different – maybe even more transient – clientele.

'75% of my customers are white,' Bansal tells me. 'We're near the Mailbox [a luxury mixed-use development that has BBC offices and luxury shops such as Harvey Nichols] and the O2 Academy. 80% of people come in for food.'

The pub is big on sports – football and cricket – and a search online reveals it's popular with sportspeople too. Test Match Special commentator Michael Vaughan enthused about the food he was served. During the 2022 Commonwealth Games there were crowds of desis coming from places like Slough and Hounslow who told Bansal they found his food compared favourably with the fare they were used to in the southeast.

Keg & Grill

Veggie mixed grill

'Grills are always at the top here,' he says. 'Women sometimes order them. It's all about the taste. Curries also go well – Punjabi lamb is very popular. It's the chef's specialty dish.'

With the veggie options and the special chef-led dishes, the Keg & Grill tries to stand out from the other desi pubs in the area. This is something Bansal admits is tricky as competition is fierce, especially during a cost-of-living crisis.

'There's too many desi pubs opening up,' he says. 'Some people who stand on the other side of the bar might think it's easy but the work that goes on behind the scenes – the preparation, getting the ingredients right – is difficult.

'The engine of the desi pub is the kitchen.'

I visited on a quiet weekday afternoon, but having come again on a busy Saturday I can say that the pub's engine works smoothly at full throttle.

Veggie mixed grill

Keg & Grill

Royal Oak

171 Holyhead Road, Birmingham B21 0BD
theroyaloakbham.co.uk
Mon–Sat 12.00–23.00; Sun 12.00–22.00.

When I spoke to food author Sejal Sukhadwala about the best way to pair
spicy food with pub drinks she mentioned that certain dishes offered by
desi pubs particularly lend themselves to be eaten tapas style. This, to me,
is the ultimate pub dining experience, because you can take your time during
your session, eating and drinking at your pace.

This isn't a new idea, and I recommend trying it with any of the starters
(or mixed grills) that I've mentioned in this book. The mogo (cassava) at the
Regency (p44) is a great example, especially if you're in a group, as a root
vegetable dish will become too filling for one. I even remember the recently
closed Windmill in Croydon calling a lot of their home-cooked dishes tapas.
Dipta Barot (the landlord's wife) would make snack-like grub, such as
samosas, in a small kitchen and serve them through a hatch. They were the
perfect complement to drinks and meant the food was on an equal footing
to the beers.

A lot of the pubs featured in this book don't market their food in this
way, though, and their menus list starters and mains separately. But this is
where a lot of the interesting personal dishes are hidden. A friend, journalist
Mark Machado, firmly believes that desi pubs 'are all about the starters'.

At the Royal Oak they've decided to adhere to Machado's mantra and
stand out under the ownership of Amrick Saini – who also runs the
Fourways in Rowley Regis (p120) – and his brother. When I spoke to Saini
about the Fourways, he kept wanting to tell me about his other pub, and in
the end drove me there because he knew I'd love it.

He wasn't exaggerating. When I open the door I come face to face with
a huge TV screen – the largest I've seen in a pub – and the walls are adorned
with beautiful Indian paintings. It feels very homely, despite being a large
venue, thronging with an interesting desi crowd who are diverse in age.

Davinder Singh

Royal Oak

When people ask me where Indians eat this is now my first thought, mainly because it's rare for the older generation to dine out *en masse* when home cooking is such a family-based traditional pursuit. Here the food is so good it becomes many desis' second home.

'I'm trying to set up a concept in the minds of people that pub food is not inferior and even better than at a good restaurant,' says chef Deepak Kumar.

'This is Saini's dream project. And he's worked very hard to make this a food and family destination.'

The pub is split in two, with the entrance – where the huge TV screen is – acting as a sports bar, while the other side is the 'restaurant' area. It even has an open-plan kitchen which can be viewed from a few tables, so the well-drilled operation becomes its own entertainment.

Despite the competing amusement of kitchen and TV screen, Kumar says that the food is king here, which is the main reason why it's so popular with British-Indians. Saini's Fourways may be 90% white, but the demographic here can be subverted, making it very diverse, especially when they open specially for coaches of travelling away fans visiting Albion, Villa or Wolves' football stadiums. Luckily for foodies, this is an itinerant crowd that only visits for a few hours before the kitchen becomes a hive of activity.

Kumar is also one of the main reasons for its success. He's a highly experienced chef who sees the Oak as his blank canvas. He creates great works using spices shipped from India and the finest quality ingredients possible.

He started working in kitchens in India in 1992 and has experience of Caribbean and Mexican cooking, as well as working in a tapas bar in Luton. Kumar's impressive CV also includes fine dining in central London and India.

He visited many desi pubs 20-odd years ago, but, being an outlier, never felt like copying the food they produced. 'I want people to copy us,' Kumar says. 'Saini is always [impelling us] to do more research. The kitchen is like a laboratory. We have over 50 spices – we have to use our minds and experiment.'

Chefs in other pubs are often are reticent, perhaps because it's hard to explain why the dishes they produce are so loved. Kumar has no such problem. He's very articulate and keen to enthuse about the beauty of his kitchen output.

'We process [cut] all our meat here,' he says, 'to control the quality.'

All the starters have different sauces and the way the plates are dressed is similar to an expensive fine-dining experience, but without the cost: starters are around £7 and tapas-style dishes are under £10. They also change the menu every 6–8 months, with input from each of the large team of chefs managed by Kumar. This means that under the tapas section there are dishes, such as Mongolin Paneer, which other Indian restaurants (or pubs) rarely serve, and which are particularly good options for diners who are vegetarian or vegan.

'Our portion sizes are not really big,' Kumar says. 'But there are certain local cultural [dishes] we have to follow. Everybody loves a mixed grill because it's a sharing platter. The difference is our mixed grill is totally different quality wise.'

'We have the best equipment to cook it and we make sure the marination lasts one and a half days. The mixed grill culture is very, very strong here.'

There's a lovely Hindi word Kumar uses to describe one of his favourite dishes he's created on the menu: *chatpata*. It means tangy and his Chatpata Wings (similar to Indo-Chinese Chicken Lollipops) are a flavour sensation – not too sour, and absolutely delectable. They taste like the best chaat (the roadside snacks you find in India) and the tangy, salty flavour is the result of combining salt (bitter) with some acidity. If Kumar's kitchen lab had a chalkboard it would probably read: sulphur + salt + acidity = chatpata.

But this isn't blind experimenting. 'When you use a spice,' he says, 'you should know exactly what the taste will be, otherwise you will not be able to control the result.'

Kumar is very good at why 'home-style' cooking – the kind of dishes our mothers produced – lingers in our memories, and why we come to desi pubs with high expectations.

'Your mother cooks with love and passion,' he says. 'It can't go wrong because [when you're young] you don't have expectations. We do the same, but in bulk, but like mother's cooking we cook with passion. We don't see our customers as customers but as guests like when someone visits my home.'

Kumar grew up with deep yellow dals, slow cooked with onions, garlic and green chilies. He was taught when he was very young by his mother that good cuisine was all about process. For example, you can't cook tasty lentils or rice unless you soak it beforehand.

'There are no shortcuts. If you take shortcuts, you will make shortcut dishes.'

This is what Saini has created at the Oak by working with Kumar to create something special. They haven't reinvented Indian food, because this type of dining, especially in its home country, is ever-evolving and open to outside influences. Instead, they've reinvented what their customers can expect when eating out.

This pub is, by whatever criteria you use, a big hitter and is producing dishes that mark it out as one of the best desi pubs in the country. If you're not local, I'd recommend making a trip here to savour some amazing 'experimental' dishes.

Royal Oak

Soho Tavern

407 Park Road, Birmingham B18 5SR
sohotavern.co.uk
Mon–Fri 12.00–23.00; Sat & Sun 11.30–23.30.

Outside of London a lot of British-Asians regard Birmingham as the capital city of desi pubs, and there's a good argument for this to be the case, especially if you include other parts of the Black Country, such as Smethwick and West Bromwich. Unlike in London, though, most people who live in the Midlands know what a desi pub is, including white pub-goers, and this inevitably leads to many differing opinions of what makes a good one.

The generally accepted quintessential components of a great desi pub are excellent Indian food, friendly owners who are enmeshed in the community, and a relaxed 'pubby' feel. I think there's another factor: serving local specialities alongside desi cuisine to create what could be deemed 'fusion food'.

In the case of the West Midlands the best example of this is chips, and this sets it apart from other parts of the country, particularly London, where you wouldn't dream of ordering this as a side dish among your mixed grills, curries or dahls.

It may seem odd to many to order chips with Indian food, but British-Indians in the Midlands love serving, and being served, different types of fries with their mixed grills, shish kebabs and curries. That's partly because the chips you're being offered are very different to the type you'll find at your local chippy.

The Soho Tavern's chili chips will convert even the strongest sceptic. Mikey Singh joins my table when my order arrives and isn't surprised by my instant love of them. They're both crispy and moist; covered in chili sauce but not in any way soggy. They don't feel greasy or unwholesome, in fact I'd go as far to say this is the ultimate desi pub soul food. I ask Singh how he manages it.

'That's a secret,' he says, laughing. 'We worked on this recipe for years. We're most famously known for our chili chips. People know of them in North America. I don't even think you can get them in India to be honest.'

Chili chips

Mikey Singh

Soho Tavern

When we're sitting down – we're lucky to get a seat as the place is full, even though it's a weekday night – I notice that a lot of people come in and order chili chips as a takeaway option, which are unbagged as soon as they go outside. It really is a phenomenon, and one that has no comparison. They don't overwhelm the dish, like curried chips from a Chinese takeaway, and nor are they overly filling. They're simply perfect.

There's a lot that's perfect about the Soho Tavern. Its fabulously lit bright bar and open diner-style tables make for great cross-party chats. In fact, I'm soon engaged with lots of people I've just met and who want to know about the book.

Regular punters travel from all around the Midlands to come here. It's particularly popular with Albion fans, who come here before the game because it's located very close to the tram stop. Singh explains the secret of their success.

'We're quite affordable,' he says. 'We offer very good quality for the price. Our spiceyness depends on the dish.'

I tell him that the chips are definitely on the hot side, and he quips, 'It's in the name! If you had had the Masala chips then they would've been on the milder side. We've even got salt and pepper ones. Because our chefs are from Nepal, they've got this pool of knowledge from China, India and their own country.'

As mentioned elsewhere, Nepalese chefs are trained to work in this country and the dishes at the Soho Tavern show they have the flexibility to adapt to British-style cuisines. I ask Singh if some dishes you'll find in Nepal will find their way on to a menu in Birmingham.

'The momos [dumplings],' says Singh, 'are eaten by the chefs in their spare time but because it's such a delicate dish and needs time it's hard to deliver in a busy environment. When it comes to the menu, we only have food we can deliver at high pressure.'

These Nepalese dumplings aren't unique to the Soho Tavern, but their own branded chili sauces, which they sell by the gallon, are. These have proved so successful that they're planning to bring out a bottled range, priced around the £3.50 mark. They're starting with a mild mint sauce, then one for seafood (which would be an Indian take on a tartare sauce) and a chutney-like relish made from red apples, which would be particularly good with a mixed grill.

Mixed grill

'A lot of [desi] pubs make this with green apples, but we find red apples to be less tangy and more full of flavour,' Singh says.

It helps to offer your customers something different if you're in the heart of the desi pub capital it seems. And with new British-Indian pubs opening all the time, Singh has to be constantly evolving his menu and adding new, intriguing items. He even has an eponymous dish on the menu called Mikey Chops.

'I love to mess around in the kitchen,' he says. 'So I once tried to create my own dish and ended up making this creamy sauce. It originally started as a soya dish called a Mikey Special. That's on the vegetarian menu and everyone loved the sauce, so we put it on the lamb chops.

'I love experimenting with food and creating new dishes. My mum was a great cook and when I was 17 or 18 I saw the talents these chefs had. I wanted to know how they did it. You think something like making a naan is simple, but it takes real talent.'

Singh feels that this kind of innovation means that his pub – and a lot of desi pubs like it – have a wide appeal which makes them more resilient to external forces, such as rising food and fuel bills. That said, he's reluctantly had to raise the prices of his mixed grills to cover some of those rising costs. But not hiking up all his prices, and sharing the burden, shows how he puts the customer first at all times.

'When you come here,' he says, 'you can ask for a dish just how you like it.'

This isn't just a perk for regulars. Bespoke dishes are on the menu and anyone can choose their base, or even decide to have their curry 'desi style' – strong on the garlic, ginger and fresh green chilies.

It's a winning formula which has seen other branches open in West Bromwich and, in June 2022, in Gateshead (the north-east is an untapped region for desi cuisine so it's a wise move). If I wanted to recommend a quintessential modern desi pub – regardless of its location – I would definitely say this Birmingham original is a fine place to start.

And you won't go wrong ordering the chips, even if that isn't the first thing you'd expect from Indian cuisine.

Soho Tavern

Fourways Bar & Grill

2 Portway Hill, Rowley Regis, B65 9DD
T 0121 559 4394
fourwaysbarandgrill.uk
Mon–Fri 14.00–23.00; Sat 12.00–23.00; Sun 12.00–22.00.

Desi pubs in the West Midlands are so commonplace – and popular – that even pockets that don't have a high proportion of South Asians will have some great establishments. Rowley Regis is one such place with its predominantly white population and traditional town feel.

The area is the highest point of the West Midlands, and, fittingly, it has a desi pub that towers over a lot of its rivals. The reason why the Fourways is so special is the friendliness of the landlord who picks me up from the train station and gives me a mini tour of the desi pubs connected to his family. (His uncle, Surjit, set up the Red Lion in West Bromwich (p148) and he also runs the Royal Oak in Birmingham (p112) with his brother).

When Saini took over the Fourways he knew the pub had a reputation for drug-dealing, racism and fights. It was not a friendly place for many people, let alone a potential new desi owner who was keen to make a mark in hospitality.

The transformation has been incredible. This isn't just a new owner who kicked out a few dodgy locals – more than 150 customers had to be ejected for life – and carried on without changing the clientele, this is a visionary who turned a crime scene into a family-friendly space. The extent to which the pub caters for its new demographic can be seen in the play area (called Paw Ways) and the fibreglass dinosaur figures that decorate the interior, making it not only a great pub but also a kind of desi Wacky Warehouse.

'It's 100% a family pub,' he says. 'The busiest time is when the kids are on holiday from school. They like the mild curries, like chicken korma.'

This transformation didn't happen overnight. Saini says it took two years to build the pub into its present form, and in 2012 Paw Ways was constructed, much to the scepticism of some of the locals. But the customers when he took over (90% white, 10% desi) knew he was the right man to turn things

around and stood shoulder-to-shoulder with him whenever any trouble was brewing.

'We had racism [when we opened],' he admits. 'But now no. It's self-policed.'

Family is a strong part of Saini's life. As are desi pubs. Surjit opened the legendary Red Lion 30-odd years ago and it was this family connection that led to Saini opening up the doors of the Fourways.

'He helped me out big time with the finances,' he says. 'I came to this country in 2002 when I was 26. My mum still lives in India. When she came to the pub she liked it a lot.'

Life wasn't easy for Saini when he arrived. He worked in an Asian supermarket in the day and in a bar at night so he could support himself while he was a student. A working day that sometimes would be as long as 20 hours.

He would stay awake drinking coffee and energy drinks, something he's never liked, and he's probably the first publican I've met who has a healthier lifestyle now he's in a pub. It is still hard work, though, and the huge kitchen pumps out an array of dishes that have to be served quickly to the families.

The pub is about to be very busy, Saini tells me, because the World Cup is about to start and the locals love to watch the football while ordering mixed grills. They're spoiled, too, as the Fourways has a massive charcoal barbeque which produces beautifully charred meat dishes, such as the chicken tikka pieces which I had.

Fourways Bar & Grill

Chicken tikka pieces

Chicken tikka pieces

Saini has four full-time chefs, and has in the past struggled to retain staff as a lot of desi pubs are opening up in the surrounding area.

The cost-of-living crisis has also impacted his business greatly. Take the BBQ I mentioned. They use about 10–12 big bags of charcoal a week, the cost of which keeps rising. Saini has had to absorb a lot of these price increases, something which he does because he believes strongly in the importance of the pub as a vital institution.

'I'm working for the local community,' he says. 'I always look after my customers. This isn't my pub – I always say it is a public house. People who eat and drink here: they own the place, not me. I'm just here to serve them.

'My job is to provide good food, drinks, a good atmosphere and a clean pub. My regular customers will come every day. I drink with them, sit down with them, and eat with them.'

It is a worry that rising fuel and food prices could affect desi pubs adversely, especially those pumping out naans and charcoal-charred skewered meats, like the Fourways, that will see their margins squeezed. And their customer base (mainly working families) will also be adversely affected by the economic situation.

But for Saini his job is a simple one for now. Keep the punters happy, the welcome warm and the food hot-ish (the curries here are generally milder because of the kids) and, hopefully, things will improve in the future.

If desi pubs fail then it really is a bellwether for the struggles that the larger pub industry faces as these businesses are popular, food-orientated destinations. For now, though, the Fourways is thriving and everyone who values community pubs will be hoping that continues, despite the economic environment.

Fourways Bar & Grill

Blue Gates Hotel

84 High Street, Smethwick B66 1AQ
T 0121 558 0389
Mon–Fri 14.00–22.30; Sat & Sun 12.00–22.30.

Out of all the pubs I've visited for this book, the Blue Gates is the best-known due to its (notorious) history, primarily because it was where US civil rights leader Malcolm X was racially discriminated against. As mentioned on p16, the US civil rights leader turned up in the mid-60s to the segregated Smethwick boozer with members of the Indian Workers Association, including Avtar Jouhl Singh, and they were all refused service on grounds of colour.

The visit, which also included Marshall Street where non-white residents were struggling to buy homes, brought national shame to Smethwick. It has to be said that a lot of this outrage was misdirected as pubs around the country were segregated, including my local in South London, which adopted racist practices until the mid 1990s when it was taken over by a Wetherspoons.

Smethwick might have been called 'Britain's most racist town' in newspaper headlines, but such prejudice was commonplace everywhere without it gaining much press attention at the time. And when it was reported (as I found out when delving into the archives), press coverage was always from the perspective of the person who was committing the offence.

But what couldn't be denied was that Malcolm X's visit was a watershed moment for anti-racism campaigners who strived to highlight how the colour bar blighted lives. The Blue Gates is a large pub, so you can see how it would have been easy to segregate customers from a practical point of view. The former smoking room did not allow entry to non-whites during Malcolm X's visit in 1965.

Today, the Blue Gates couldn't be further from a segregated pub. It's now West Bromwich Albion's official boozer, according to the pub's owner, and will fill up with fans before and after home matches – even during midweek when other pubs that are nearer the Hawthorns don't see an uptick in business.

Jatinder 'Jat' Singh's father took over the pub in 1977 and Jat runs it with his brother, Narinder, who works here part-time. They make an odd pairing: while Narinder is a larger-than-life character, Jat is a more considered, calming – almost shy – presence. Both, though, are lovely people. On one visit before a West Bromwich Albion game, Jat was asking supporters how their week had been and working his avuncular charm on the children.

Unlike the other pubs in this book, food isn't a big thing here, though there are cobs (Black Country-style in a container on the bar) and Indian snacks such as samosas and spicy chicken wings. I highly recommend having a few pints of Mild here and then walking round the corner for a curry or sizzling platter at the Red Cow (p130), or taking a longer walk in the other direction to the Ivy Bush (p126) for some modern Indian-Nepalese treats.

As mentioned elsewhere, Mild is popular with British-Indians of an older vintage, and here's it's £2.50 a pint – possibly the cheapest outside of a Spoons (or supermarket).

'Having said that,' Jat says. 'There's a boy called Bobby who comes in and drinks it. He's about 30s or 40s. We don't sell as much as Carling. In the Midlands we're known for our Mild.'

Jat admits that his dad was brave when taking over the pub, 'Because there were hardly any Indian pubs in those days. One or two.' That's all he has to say on the subject, however. He's proud of the pub nowadays and doesn't want to dwell on its history.

The Blue Gates may have changed radically in terms of its clientele and atmosphere since Malcolm X's visit back in the 1960s, but many things have stayed the same. It looks and feels like a wonderfully well-preserved working man's club; like a window to the past, but without any of the racism, prejudice or aggro.

Here, life is peaceful – unless someone puts on the jukebox while West Bromwich Albion are on the TV.

Jat Singh

Blue Gates Hotel

Ivy Bush

218 St Paul's Road, Smethwick B66 1QS
T 0121 293 3882 · theivybushkitchen.com
Pub: *Sun–Thu 12.00–23.00; Fri & Sat 12.00–24.00.*
Kitchen: *Mon–Thu 16.00–22.00; Fri & Sat 14.00–22.30; Sun 14.00–22.00.*

Lakhbir (Lacky) Singh is very proud of the multicultural make-up of his Smethwick pub which he runs with his son. It shows how desi pubs like this one have been crucial in soothing the town's traumatic history of prejudice. This is especially telling as the Ivy Bush stands next to Marshall Street, the road visited by Malcolm X in the mid-60s, where non-white residents suffered racism when they tried to buy property. There's now a blue plaque nearby marking the civil rights leader's appearance, and a stained-glass window in the Red Lion in West Bromwich (see p148).

'Not sure if people call my pub a desi pub,' Singh says. 'But it's quite diverse. There's no racial tension. All sorts of people come here. All ages. Young kids come with their parents up to 80-year-olds. So it's quite mixed.

'I run things differently to other pubs,' Singh says. 'I like my customers to know each other by name and I introduce them to each other. Even if you hadn't visited for a few months everybody would know your first name.

'When I used to go to pubs, as soon as I walked through the door people would stare at me [...] but I didn't give a monkey's. I went to places like Kidderminster and I was the only Asian. You could cut the tension with a knife.'

Singh decided to create something very different and took over the pub in the 1990s. It was tricky at first as a barman was stealing from him, but he pragmatically kept him on so that he could learn how a cellar worked. In those days there was no food, but, when the smoking ban kicked in, he started selling tandoori chicken from a tent outside in 2003.

'We first employed a proper chef in 2007,' he says. 'Now everybody wants to eat Indian food. It makes me laugh because [...] people would complain that I smelt of garlic.'

Being a veteran, he is happy to talk about when the phrase desi pubs first

Ivy Bush

started to become widely used. 'The South Bank Show showed pubs serving mixed grills. I first heard the word when someone started buying pubs and calling them Desi Island and [Desi Junction in West Brom, now closed]. "Desi" means Asian culture.'

When I started working on this book I went to the Ivy and I told Singh that I had a Sikh friend who lived in Yorkshire who claimed desi pubs were pubs that 'Indians drank in', and if they were frequented by white people they weren't 'authentic'. Singh shook his head and said he was wrong, insisting it's to do with 'mixed grills, curries', and how Asian people have stamped their mark on the pub. Ever since that conversation I've used Singh's criteria. If you disagree you can take it up with him.

Ivy Bush

I can see why my Yorkshire friend held that theory, though. It's easy to be obsessed with this idea of authenticity, but when it comes down to the logistics, creating an inclusive environment is perhaps the most authentic way of running a pub. You're not chasing a particular demographic, which can be dangerous, especially during a cost-of-living crisis.

The Ivy used to specialise in Indian 'staples' – the soothing curries, the sizzling mixed grills. Recently, though, Singh has changed everything around by employing a Nepalese chef whose dishes, such as momos, have earned rave reviews from all the customers. The Soho Tavern in Birmingham (see p83) also has Nepalase chefs, but found they couldn't produce momos as they're too tricky to produce in mass quantities.

Here – and in the Fishponds Tap in Bristol (p116) – they're a tapas-like delicacy that goes well with beer, and in the saturated desi pub market of Smethwick/West Brom they offer customers something different. They also do mixed grills but some of their dishes are unfamiliar – a few customers of Jamaican origin were loving the Everest goat curry on my most recent visit.

The kitchen is a separate business to the pub, so you order and pay the chef directly. I ask for sea bass and chips. Obviously, this was cooked desi-style

Sea bass and chips

Ivy Bush

with a deep Indian spice rub but it was absolutely glorious, and during a long weekend where I was offered plenty of mixed grills and spiced meats, it was a welcome diversion.

It was also refreshing to have plain chips – I've had chili chips, masala chips, even butter chicken chips (just the sauce) – because fish would be overpowered by the various flavours and a deep sauce. Sometimes it's good to pare down the ingredients and let the cooking be simple, especially if it's bespoke.

And that's actually how Singh runs the pub: simple but bespoke. He once told me he could've branched out and opened other boozers, but he's at the age – 63 – where there's no point in trying to create something new when you do the old stuff so well.

'You know that American programme *Cheers*?' Singh asks. 'Well, my pub is like that: "everybody knows your name".'

Every time I visit Smethwick, it is great to see the old faces. I've managed to become a local in a town that's hundreds of miles from where I live. Take my word for it: visit the three pubs I've featured in Smethwick and they'll (and you'll) be glad you came.

Red Cow

296 High Street, Smethwick B66 3NL
T 0121 558 0272
Pub: *Mon–Sun 12.00–23.00.*
Kitchen: *Mon–Sun 12.00–22.30.*

Because of its history as a town that went from being a battleground of racism to a post-prejudice beacon, it's easy for me to romanticise the Black Country town of Smethwick.

The past was so bleak for desis living here that it seems incomprehensible that the town's pubs are now virtually all owned by British-Indians. For someone like me, seeking proof that a post-racist world is possible, then Smethwick is my Wakanda (for those of you not familiar, it's the self-sufficient fictional nation in Black Panther).

But it's important to remind ourselves of a shocking past. From the 1950s, Punjabi workers moved from India to Smethwick to work in the town's foundries that serviced the car industry. Conditions were gruelling as the factories were Victorian buildings without proper ventilation and accidents were common.

To make matters worse, racism and segregation was rife: inside the workplace, on the street, and, pertinently in the pubs. It was common for brown workers to be paid less than their white counterparts – despite being employed to do the more dangerous work – and to have to endure the indignity of separate factory toilets.

Pubs were even worse. The Blue Gates (p123) and the now-closed Wagon and Horses were two examples of the many inns operating the colour bar. At the Wagon and the Gates non-whites were barred from various smoking rooms and lounge bars where they were told that the customers hated them speaking in Punjabi.

It was argued by landlords – then most pubs were run by Mitchells and Butler – that it was a 'squalor bar', but there was evidence that it wasn't just factory workers of colour who faced prejudice; doctors and teachers of Indian origin were also segregated.

Things got so bad that anti-racist campaigners like Avtar Singh Jouhl enlisted the help of Malcolm X to show the world how much prejudice British-Asians faced (see p18). Jouhl is one of Smethwick's heroes – who died recently – and he earns this status through a lifetime of anti-racism campaigning that eventually led to him being awarded an OBE.

His tactic, which was part of a campaign by the Indian Workers' Association, was to visit pubs with some white students and note down those in which he was refused service. He would then wait until the landlords' licences came up for renewal and give evidence against them. Often, they would be replaced by British-Indian landlords and his legacy lives on today in the town's many desi pubs. Even the Blue Gates, where Jouhl took Malcolm X (both were refused service in the lounge bar) is now a desi pub.

I cannot emphasise enough the mark Jouhl has left on Smethwick and desi pub culture. This book would not exist without him.

I visit the Red Cow one Monday morning with Avtar's son, Jagwant. We're here to meet the pub's veteran landlord Bera Mahli who is 'running 10 minutes late' as he's travelling from his son's pub in Evesham (p87). The barman jokes and says 10 minutes to Mahli is 20 minutes to everyone else, so we sit down and sup an M&B Mild, which is now contract brewed by Molson Coors.

At the bar is a desi who is visiting his hometown after moving to Stourbridge. He misses the pubs a lot and finds where he lives a bit too cliquey, especially when he walks into a pub.

Mahli then bursts through the door in a whirlwind of grey hair and enthusiasm for all things Smethwick, despite his 65 years, and recent kidney problems. He mentions that desi pubs weren't that well known as a phrase until Desi Junction opened, a rowdy Black Country pub that often was packed with all types of drinkers.

Red Cow

Bera Mahli

131

Jagwant Johal

Mahli himself is a desi landlord trailblazer. He was the first Smethwick publican to realise that there was a huge potential customer base in the Albion fans on match days. He had run the Redfort Social Club from 1999 and 'turned it into a desi pub' cooking Punjabi food.

'There was one other publican,' he tells us. 'But they weren't as popular and even Lacky [at the Ivy Bush, p126] wasn't doing food then.'

The Redfort could only serve about 40 people at one time so you can see why Mahli moved to the Red Cow with its huge open-plan seating area. The only problem was how to attract the football fans as the Red Cow is located a substantial walk to the Hawthorns, which hadn't been an issue in the Redfort.

'We've got our own taxi firm!' he laughs. 'It's an incentive: you come here and we will get you to the ground. Now on match day they come early at 11am and at 2pm we get them free of charge to the ground.'

It's a special pub. And these supporters who are chauffeured to the ground get to enjoy the massive mixed grills of marinated prawns, chops and wings. The tandoor regularly churns out naan and the drink flows.

But that's not the only standout feature of the Red Cow, which also embraces the fine Punjabi traditions of kabaddi and bhangra. Mahli himself was in a bhangra band and this gives the pub a unique and vibrant fusion of Britishness and Punjabi culture.

Mahli, like a lot of the veteran Black Country landlords, is used to adapting to suit the ever-changing nature of the area. His very first boozer was called the Cock Inn and in the 1980s he used to serve thirsty desis who worked in the foundries on their lunch breaks.

'At lunchtime,' he remembers, 'I would fill the bar with half-filled pints of Mild. Get the change ready and then they would have a couple of pints and go back and have their roti.'

The Red Cow's mixed grill is said to be one of the best examples in the country, and it certainly is a sizzling delight to behold. Like Mahli, it is larger than life, and perfect, even if you're not taking one of his taxis to the match afterwards.

Tap & Tandoor

658 Warwick Road, Solihull B91 3DX
https://tapandtandoor.co.uk
Monday 16.00–23.00; Tue–Thu 12.00–23.00;
Fri & Sat 12.00–24.00; Sun 12.00–22.00.

Solihull has a distinct identity that marks it out from surrounding urban sprawl of Birmingham. It's a market town with a thriving high street with department stores such as John Lewis, and even has a desi pub, the Tap & Tandoor, which aims to offer something different.

Publican Ajay Kenth doesn't even like the term desi pub and feels it's more suitable to call his venue an Indian gastropub, something I'm slightly uncomfortable with. My personal experience – based on the part of south-east London where I live – is that gastropubs haven't exactly enriched the pub scene because they've courted casual diners (especially mid-range restaurant goers) at the expense of beer lovers who just want a good ale and a chat. They offer expensive meals but few beer options, and, moreover, lack a diverse clientele.

Ajay Kenth

But maybe my local experience of a gastropub has left me with an unconscious bias, one that needs to be challenged in order to enjoy a pub that is a modern adaptation of many of the ones I've lovingly featured in this book. Especially because beer is king here, as the huge offering of keg and cask lagers and pale ales proves, and the way the food has been carefully chosen to pair well with the meals.

It's a busy Friday night when I arrive in time to watch a football match. All tables are full so I'm lucky to get a seat. You can come here just for a drink, but everyone seems to be ordering dishes to go with their beers. The staff

are attentive, though, and there's table service as well as at the bar. First up, I put the tapas-style menu to the test and order Amritsari fish and okra fries.

The fish is very lightly battered and complemented by caraway seeds, which goes well with the Purity Session IPA I have; the grapefruit-y notes of the beer really hangs together with the soft fish.

The okra fries are lightly dusted in gram flour and I'm pleasantly surprised by a light crunch, while the inside of the snack isn't slimy (which I find a recurring problem). In fact, when I've had okra fries before I've regretted the order, unless I'm sharing them in a group, but here it's a perfect dish to start the meal.

Towards the end of the night the hubbub dies down and Kenth joins me at the table. He's keen to explain how everything here has a plan, especially the bar layout, which has all the taps behind the bar staff.

'In a traditional bar,' he says, 'you always have the taps in front of you. I see that as a barrier to communication. We sell Carling, Peroni, Aspall [cider] and Guinness but the amount of people we've converted from Carling to Belgium pilsners is phenomenal.

'I present it well in a tankard and they go "wow!" We do get Carling drinkers, but we like to educate people about craft.'

Four of their beers rotate on a weekly basis so there's plenty for the non-Carling drinkers to choose from and this allows Kenth the opportunity to trial beers from around the country and even do mini tap takeovers. The town has one other craft pub – the Indian Brewery Company had an outlet but it closed – but the attention to beer selection marks it out compared to 90% of British-Indian pubs.

That's not to say this is a captive craft market, as two giant Wetherspoons next to each other attests. But Kenth is hugely trusted to create a bespoke, and in many ways novel experience for his customers. 'I went to school with a lot of them,' he says.

'When I was growing up we never ate out in Solihull, we went to the Vine in West Brom. I remember saying to my dad "why do we have to travel so far? Why can't we have a place like that here?"'

Creating an institution like the Vine is a bold venture because, as I mentioned (see p152) that pub underwent decades of evolution before it turned into the first modern food and beer destination in the Midlands area. But it's something Kenth is well equipped to achieve, especially because he has experience already in changing an area's food landscape.

Before T&T he set up an Indian street food bar with his wife, Shivani, in Moseley called Zindiya, which serves a mixture of snacks, such as pani puri

Okra fries

Amritsari fish

Purity Session IPA

Tap & Tandoor

(wheat balls filled with potatoes, onions and chickpeas served with coriander and tamarind chutneys), dosas and modern adaptations of chicken tikka.

'We looked at this place,' Kenth says, 'and thought "how much different can this be to a restaurant?" We soon found out it was very different. But I thought "why can't an Indian pub be a gastropub?" Because "gastro" means quality and everything here is about quality.'

The quality Kenth talks about manifests itself in the food sourcing and sustainability, as well as making sure the dishes they serve are novel. Kenth and his wife regularly visit other food outlets to gain inspiration. He also applies this philosophy to the beer. He aims to work with the best brewers who produce beers that can be paired well with the food that his kitchen painstakingly produces.

But it's also the minor details in his pub which are important to him.

'The pub has to be warm [through] lighting, music and a fireplace. And it has to be a hub of the community – people coming here just for a chat and a drink.

'My children eat here – my daughter loves the butter chicken. Good pub food has to be soul food.'

Here heat levels can be tinkered with, but only if it works with a specific dish, so Kenth will tell someone (or in his words 'educate' them) that having a chili-heavy butter chicken would ruin the taste. The default of the heat levels are mid-range and it's a very family-friendly environment, even with beers flowing freely for punters, like me, who are watching the football.

I'm then joined by Shivani who tells me how much the atmosphere has changed over the years. She has a hand in this pub business – there are other Tap & Tandoors in Peterborough and Southampton – and, apart from Meg in the Glad (see p68), I think she's the nearest I've come to finding a desi pub 'landlady' on my recent travels.

Like Meg, she's involved in the operation of an establishment that is updating what we can expect from an Indian-run boozer, and what she tells me about old-style desi pubs resonates with other women's experiences. Her father would drink in Spark Hill Social Club on Friday with other men despite it being next door to a community club where the whole family went.

'As a kid,' she tells me, 'we couldn't even go to the door to see our dads.'

Excluding entire sections of a family from a pub is a very risky business model and it's ironic that nearly every desi pub landlord I've spoken to took over a boozer that was failing. The T&T has embraced the whole community but is willing to 'educate' their locals as to how modern Indian food can be evolving, paired with craft and eaten like tapas.

I even think it's changed my mind about gastropubs.

Lazy Hill Tavern

196 Walsall Wood Road, Walsall WS9 8HB
Pub: Mon–Fri 16.00–23.00; Sat 12.00–23.00; Sun 12.00–22.30.
Kitchen: Mon–Thu 16.00–21.30; Fri 16.00–22.00; Sat 14.00–22.00; Sun 12.00–21.30.

In some parts of the UK people might think that a mixed grill is the kind of plain meat fest you'd find at a Harvester pub chain, but in Aldridge, Walsall, the proximity to West Bromwich means everyone knows desi pub food. Which means there's a captive audience for excellent fare served up in a welcoming environment by a second generation British-Indian.

When I first enter the Lazy Hill I walk back out as I'm certain I'm in the wrong place. 'Where are you looking for, duck?' A middle-aged woman asks me. I tell her breathlessly that I'm after a desi pub run by Sodhy Singh, son of Dalwinder at the Island Inn (p140). 'This is it, duck!'

Inside, the Tudor-style beams, low ceilings and bar full of people drinking fine ales paint a bucolic picture of a gentle village pub. This is the kind of pub I really love, so long as the locals are friendly and the staff are welcoming. But no one is eating Indian food here and I'm convinced it's an elaborate hoax. Maybe Dalwinder, who told me about this place, has an odd sense of humour?

I ask the bartender if Singh works here and she tells me to 'go out back'. I walk through a door behind the bar expecting a kitchen and then it hits me: the total opposite of the village pub. A light-filled space – thanks to the Red Lion-inspired retractable roof – with desi staff tending to a large kitchen and serving pints with sizzling grills. I finally meet Singh and he smiles.

'This used to be an old ballroom,' he says. 'It was an empty room. The bar area is completely separate – it's for my drinkers, my regulars. People of the local area who come to the pub for community, for the decor (the beams) and for how it's a traditional English pub.

'So we kept that theme and served food in this space.'

Singh took over the pub in 2019 before lockdown and two years later he renovated the 'ballroom'. The previous owner ran the pub well but was retiring and had succession issues. Unlike many desi pubs, this wasn't a failing business and Singh was very savvy to jump in and turn it to a cross-cultural venue.

'My dad has been in the pub game,' he says, 'for 30-odd years. I've been working with him from a very young age – finishing school and washing glasses. It's second nature to me.'

When I say to Singh that he's grown up in a pub, he corrects me, quite rightly, and says he's grown up around people. This clarification is important as we often think of the logistics of learning the pub trade rather than what's really important: i.e., the social and interpersonal skills one can pick up. It's no surprise that children of desi landlords come across as wise, knowledgeable, and, above all, affable.

'I know how to engage with every type of person,' he says. 'Someone's that pleasant. Not pleasant.'

Singh's mum, Sarbjitkaur, helps out with the day-to-day running of the place – HR, that kind of thing – which leaves him to deal with the front-of-house and strategy. He's excellent at both – when I leave he works the 'drinkers' bar' seamlessly on a busy Friday evening – and is very good at finding ways to make his offering different to his competitors. Not that he sees them as rivals.

'We're a community,' he says, 'who are all growing the desi pub field. [Desi pubs] are dense in the West Brom/Smethwick area – why not branch out? Wetherspoons branched out around the country, which is a very similar thing to a desi pub but just within its own [style] of chain.

'A desi pub in a sense is a chain. It's under different brands but it's the same concept. I think desi pubs have made their mark within the whole pub industry. Everyone knows if they go to a desi pub they can get a good meal and the pub will look nice because people have invested a lot of time and money into them.

'The experience we gained,' says Singh, 'from the renovation [at the Island Inn] gave us knowledge and the ability to improve and master our craft – which is why this looks the way it does. I like the idea of having the drinking area separate and it really works on a night like tonight where we're fully booked.

'If anyone hasn't booked, I can get them to wait at the bar and get them when a table becomes available.'

It's also a very inclusive environment, with groups of women enjoying birthday celebrations, but Singh keeps the atmosphere relaxed for casual diners by seating these more boisterous groups together.

And when it comes to the food it's a real treat. The butter chicken is delicately flavoured but perfectly balanced, with a soft, home-cooked feel to the meat. The sauce is mild – as you'd expect – but manages to be both light and creamy. I also have the Indo-Chinese Chili Chicken which has a sweet sauce drenched over the crispy chicken. Both are soothing to a head that was discombobulated by walking into this village desi pub.

At the other side of the bar where the locals sit, I feel welcome as Singh works the room. The boy who branched out from West Bromwich has brought his distinct desi culture to this small town.

Lazy Hill Tavern

Sodhy Singh

139

Island Inn

2 Kenrick Way, West Bromwich B70 6BB
islandinnwestbromwich.co.uk
Mon–Sat 12.00–23.00; Sun 12.00–22.00.

When the Indian diaspora arrived in the Black Country after India partitioned in 1947, they were here to work hard and to find opportunities that were unavailable in Asia. The reality they faced – tough conditions in factories or foundries, less pay than their white counterparts, and, of course, a lot of racism – is an identifiable and personal story for many members of the Commonwealth.

My parents were part of this generation with both arriving from the then-Malaya peninsula to work in an NHS psychiatric hospital in Hertford-shire. The hours were long, the patients were racist and when they first arrived they lived in a cold static home in an unwelcoming St Albans. My dad drifted in and out of jobs, my mother remained a nurse until her retirement. Many others suffered the same fate, but some found that the opportunities in this country could give them a better life.

Places such as West Bromwich didn't seem to offer much social mobility decades ago to those who arrived without money or education, but in those days you could work hard, save money and then acquire a business like the Island Inn.

'I came here 31 March 1988,' says Dalwinder Singh, who was born in Jalandhar, in Punjab. 'I had no qualifications. I couldn't speak much English. I was a labourer in a warehouse and in the foundry. I got laid off and in 1992 I [drove a] taxi for five years. I then went into the pub trade.'

His first boozer was the Lewisham Arms in Wolverhampton. Soon after, a friend bought the Island, which was tied to Banks's brewery. Now it's a freehouse. In 2005 Dalwinder purchased the Island from his friend and hasn't looked back. He fostered a close relationship with his customers and they hold him in high regard.

Garlic naan

'The Midlands,' he says, 'especially the Black Country, is a very multi-cultural society. And we live very close to each other. I've been here nearly 23 years and I've hardly had any problems. And since we've done the place up the community appreciate it. I've done something where you can bring your family, sit in a nice environment and have nice food.'

'Before, it was the Trinity Working Men's Club,' Singh says. 'Back in the day it was whites only.' This was common practice in those days. The nearby Handsworth Horticultural Institute was taken to court in the late 1980s for operating a colour bar, despite people of colour making up 60% of the population at that time. Today, ironically, 60% of customers at the Island Inn are white. It used to have a higher proportion of desi customers, but the food is so good that people from all around the Midlands will travel here.

I suspect the Island Inn name is ironic because it's located on a round-about, and I'd recommend driving to the pub. You can walk – as I did – but it involves a short stretch on a pavement along a dual carriageway. When you arrive here, though, it's an oasis of calm. The circulating traffic may be noisy, but you wouldn't know that from inside when you sit in comfortable seats taking in its relaxed vibe.

When Singh first ran the pub it was 'like a shed', he says, but he has since extended it so there's a large open-plan bar and a bright dining area.

Island Inn

Mushroom balti

On the day the 2010 World Cup started he demolished the existing building and it was rebuilt in 14 weeks to its present state at a cost of more than £100,000.

The previous kitchen was small, only serving food in the evenings from a much smaller menu, mainly grills and curries. Nowadays, there are three chefs, all pumping out sizzling dishes and bespoke curries, which can be tailored to your taste – mild, medium, hot or Punjabi. I order a mushroom balti (medium) which I find very hot. I suspect Punjabi might be too hot for most, especially Singh, who tells me he has his food on the mild side.

The balti is really good – nourishing, gingery and very light, with no grease. The mushrooms are obviously high-quality as their flavour is able to stand out amongst the heat and spice. They're tender, like slow-cooked meat, but still retaining their bite and fragrancy. The garlic naan is crispy and not at all doughy. It's clear to see why people travel here; it's a food destination, and an interesting, comforting venue.

It's the attention to detail, too, which is down to Singh. He offers a warm welcome and is a familiar, pleasing presence to his customers, even though only around 10% of them live nearby. Because so many travel from a distance,

Dalwinder Singh

he's on hand to explain all the dishes and to ensure everyone is happy with their meals.

He works incredibly hard, like most successful pub landlords, but looks very good for his 58 years (probably because he's a keen marathon runner).

It's good to meet a veteran publican who's flourishing and enjoying every day of their job. I wonder if serving a majority of white customers and being a successful business in Britain has changed his identity towards his birth country.

'I am Indian,' he says. 'I'm never going to lose my identity. My family's here, I'm a British citizen. Nationality doesn't matter. What doesn't change is I'm still Punjabi. "Mr Singh" – that's my identity. I wear a turban quite a lot.'

His work ethic has been passed on to his son, Sodhy, who runs the Lazy Hill in Walsall (see p137) and who has continued the family pub dynasty. One troubling note in the Singh story is the cost-of-living crisis which has seen staple ingredients such as oil skyrocket in a way that means he can't pass the cost on to his customers. He also had another pub in Quinton – also called the Island, and also by a roundabout – which had to shut during the lockdown.

But this Island still stands as a monument to hard work, grasped opportunity and social harmony.

Prince of Wales

130 High Street, West Bromwich B70 6JJ
T 0121 525 6366
Open daily from 11.00 till very late.

In the heart of West Brom is a desi pub with so much character that it's like no other boozer in this country. It provides a unique experience for British-Asians, curious Indian tourists and, of course, the non-desi community. In an area where there are so many desi pubs to choose from, this one is the one that stands out for offering a totally different experience.

While other Indian-influenced pubs might try to have elements of 'home', like the Scotsman's Punjabi paintings paying tribute to Sikh heroes, the Prince of Wales is like a building that's been shrink-wrapped and shipped in from India without being touched by any British influence (apart from the drinks). It claims to be the truest desi pub in the country.

One night I was there I glanced up and saw the fans, which were part of the light fittings hanging from the ceiling. These were exactly like the type that my parents had in their bedroom, and which I thought were ridiculous growing up in Bedfordshire in the 80s and 90s, before we had summers of record-breaking temperatures. Odds and ends remind me of Asia and trinkets in my dad's family's apartments in Singapore, coffee houses in Malaysia and family friends' houses in North London.

The PoW has many features like this. Old bottles. Photos. The woven tapestry on the bar. It's often visited by Indian students and British-Indians from around the country, and it's a retro-nostalgia that's part of landlord Jinder Birring Singh's DNA. 'When people first come here,' he tells me, 'I tell them this is a proper desi pub. Punjabi style.'

What marks Singh out from every landlord (white or desi) I've come across is that he's not just a performer behind the bar – he can produce a star turn on stage. During music events, which are usually held on a Saturday night, he will play the single-string tumbi – famous in this country thanks to songs like Missy Elliott's 'Get Ur Freak On' – and sing.

And, boy, can he sing. His voice is so strong, truthful and melodic it transcends language – I don't speak Punjabi – and it completely enthralled me. I visited on a dank, cold Saturday night when the featured Punjabi singer was late and the crowd was growing restless. Arguments between the Indian students and Ray (Singh's nephew) who was working hard behind the bar showed the difference between desi Black Country and visiting cultures.

A young Indian student wanted a beer without a head, even though that's not how it's done here. The discord ended, though, as soon as the music started and Singh, dressed all in black like a desi Johnny Cash, took to the stage with the band.

The diversity of ages in the group was at odds with the watching crowd, which was young and 100% male (the pub is normally not so mono-cultured). They had been treated to free food in the back room – rice, naans, dal and chicken curry (desi-style of course, with butter-soft meat) – and the laughter, clapping and dancing began. It turned into a long night, though I left before the revelry ended (at two in the morning).

It's not normally like this, of course. Usually, the pub is a great hub for West Brom fans, food lovers and hard-drinking desis – one guy, who claims to be Singh's best friend, struggles to remember me each time I come, despite us having had cordial chats numerous times. 'He can't remember yesterday, let alone last month,' Singh admitted.

Jinder Birring Singh

It's become a hub for me whenever I visit. Singh calls any landlords he knows who he thinks would be good for me to interview. He's also driven me to pubs he thinks should be featured, such as Glassy Junction in Wolverhampton.

He's very proud of his car (a black jeep, which everyone waves at as we drive past) and of the money he raises for Indian charities. He gets this collective responsibility from his father who was a member of the Indian Workers Association, like Avtar Singh Jouhl (p18).

'He worked at the Bir-Mid foundry,' he says. 'He was friends with Avtar. Well, most of the Asian community was.'

When Singh finished school, he worked in a factory making streetlamps, but he says it wasn't as hard as working in a foundry, like his father had done. He interrupts our interview and leads me to the old, fading photos on the wall where he's pictured travelling the world.

You would think that this kind of restlessness meant that Singh isn't focused on the present or on West Bromwich, but the PoW is firmly embedded in the local neighbourhood. I speak to a few of the non-desi locals, like Elaine Maher, who is hugely grateful for their contribution to the High Street.

'Without the Asian community,' she tells me, 'a lot of these pubs just wouldn't be here. We're in our 60s and we remember the pubs back in the day – they would be really working-class pubs where people worked in the local manufacturing industry.

'The manufacturing industry has gone. These pubs serve us in a different way particularly during match days and they bring money into the local economy. We're really grateful to the Asian people who take on these pubs and do them up.

'We love coming in here during the week and having a meal. We eat out at desi pubs on a regular basis. In fact, we're going tonight but we haven't chosen which one yet.'

Elaine's husband, Paul, had a father who worked in the foundries and he remembers how different the food was then. 'It was chip butties on the bar!'

The meals in 2023 in the Prince of Wales are a bit different to other pubs in the area, mainly because their served through a hatch into a canteen-style dining area. The dishes are recognisable and there's nothing here that is radical; it's reliable, comforting, desi-style food.

You can eat at the bar area too, but having a separate canteen gives the PoW a very rustic, Punjabi feel and makes it different to the other pubs in West Brom and Smethwick, which have been revamped to feel very modern.

The PoW manages to be retro but tidy – cool even. Which is exactly how I would describe its owner.

Prince of Wales

Red Lion

190 All Saints Way, West Bromwich B71 1RH
redlionwestbrom.com
Bar: *Mon–Thu 12.00–22.00; Fri & Sat 12.00–23.00; Sun 12.00–21.30.*
Kitchen: *12.00–21.15; Fri & Sat 12.00–22.00; Sun 12.00–21.00.*

West Bromwich has so many food options it can be hard to choose where to eat. As well as a slew of desi pubs, there are many restaurants, balti houses and cafés offering Asian and Caribbean fare. I've visited several times and left one of the town's most famous pubs till last, mainly because I knew I didn't want to rush – I wanted to savour every moment.

The publican of the Red Lion, Satnam Purewal, realises he has to compete, and does things very differently in his establishment, which was one of the first – and most culturally important – desi pubs in the area.

'We've become a hub [of desi pubs],' he says. 'People travel here. Because of that the standards of food have got to be really, really high.'

Purewal's father, Jeet, set up the pub in 1997, after following the example of Suki (with whom he's best friends) at the nearby Vine (see p152) by taking over a drinkers' bar that had mainly a white clientele. He had to win them over, of course, and he did so deftly, proving once again that British-Indians were well-suited to running pubs and that they could turn 'wary' customers into friends.

Asking Purewal about his experience you get a nuanced, considered view, not only because he grew up in an area that evolved from one of racial prejudice, to tolerance, to celebrating other cultures, but also because he worked at a secondary school teaching sociology and psychology (he still teaches one day a week as well as running the pub).

'A lot of times,' he says about white people's initial prejudice, 'it's because they've never known anyone from that background. When you have a drink with someone, spend the evening with them, your inhibitions go out of the window and you get to know them properly.

'Pubs create social cohesion. And that's the best thing about them.'

Visiting the Red Lion was a moving experience for me, not just because

Shema Rozario and Hari Patel

of Purewal's philosophy but because it's a shrine to the past with its gorgeous stained glass windows commemorating Malcolm X's appearance on Smethwick's Marshall Street (see p17) and the toil of the Indian diaspora when they first arrived to work in the Midland's foundries.

This was my first visit to the area since Avtar Singh Jouhl's death, and having written his obituary for *The Guardian* it felt like a full stop to my research into his great life, one that ultimately led to the region's desi pubs being set up.

However, I wasn't expecting the pub to be so forward-looking and such a warm, welcoming environment. It's a family-friendly venue for all members of the community, meticulously planned to suit everyone's needs. It even has a quiet room for autistic children.

This, Purewal tells me, was because of the time he had to reconfigure the Red Lion when Covid struck. It wasn't a refurbishment as such – that had already happened in 2017 – but rather a way of changing the business to make things ultra-safe for his customers. All these changes are in place today because they help the pub to be an inclusive environment for women and children.

'It forced us to change,' he admits. 'We couldn't squeeze in people anymore. We had to have two-metre gaps for social distancing including blocking off some urinals, table service and every month we sanitised everywhere with fogging agents. I took Covid so seriously and I was so strict. To be honest, the stricter we were being, the more people appreciated it. So it drew in a lot of trade.

Red Lion

'None of our regulars got Covid. We kept the table service, but you can still order at the bar – we're still a pub. But because 99% of our customers are families they order at the table and this helps women who might feel intimidated by a bar because of male gaze.'

Purewal also has a large room with a retractable roof – which inspired the one in Sollihul's Lazy Hill – which meant that people could eat indoors but be Covid friendly. The pandemic might have had devastating consequences, but here it was the engine house of change with the outdoor seating now being perfect for diners and drinkers on a summer's day.

Whatever the case, Purewal is the quintessential host and I feel like I can ask him questions that other publicans would feel wary about answering. The pub, aside from its great work in the pandemic – which also included a lot of charity initiatives like helping the homeless – does so much for its community, such as sponsoring children's football teams so they become freely available for all. I put it to him that being a landlord must be an empowering position for a British-Indian.

'I'm very proud to be a landlord,' he answers. 'Being in charge of your own business is always empowering. [The community work] is also a bit of a Sikh thing. It's *sevadar*, which is embedded in us. To do *sevadar* means you are giving back to the community.'

Purewal shows me around the pub and it's apparent he sees the building as an extension of his classroom, with lots of books present. He's proud that the only untidiness is the kiddie's books section. 'It shows they're used,' he beams.

When we get to the stained glass windows, he points to one which has his dad featured on it and explains why pints of Mild are so culturally important to the older generation who worked in the foundries. I knew they were drunk on their lunch breaks, but until now I never knew why factory workers took to Mild with such enrthusiasm.

'They used to get all this rubbish on their chest,' he says about the polluted, inhumane conditions. 'Because Mild was a very weak beer it would clear it out.

'Not many youngsters drink it now. But if we get people visiting from London who lived in the Midlands and they see the [Banks's] Mild on the tap they go "whoa! I've got to have one of those!" It's nostalgia for people who live elsewhere.'

The only thing I regret about my trip to the Red Lion is Purewal's Tigger-like energy meant he had to leave before I could ask him for his photograph. Next time.

The highly competitive food that he mentioned wasn't hype. I have a sizzling salmon tikka dish which is crispy on the outside but succulent in the middle. It's a tricky dish to pull off as the onions and red peppers could normally overpower the salmon but it holds together really well. It's great for sharing and a bit much for one, despite my gallant efforts.

I also ordered a tarka dhal which is as comforting as Purewal's words. I watch how his customers – both desi and white – warmly greet the hardworking staff and how they feel saddened to have missed Purewal. I'm left with the feeling of having been in the presence of a great mind who could articulate exactly why desi pubs are such a powerful force of social cohesion.

Red Lion

Vine

152 Roebuck Street, West Bromwich B70 6RD · T 0121 553 2866
Bar: Mon & Tue 16.00–22.00; Wed & Thu 12.00–14.00, 16.00–22.00;
    Fri & Sat 12.00–22.30; Sun 12.00–21.30.
Kitchen: Mon & Tue 16.00–22.00; Wed & Thu 12.00–14.00, 16.00–22.00;
    Fri 12.00–22.00; Sat 13.00–22.00; Sun 13.00–21.30.

Desi pubs in the Black Country started out as places that British-Indian workers in the foundries and factories could visit when other establishments were hostile or imposed segregation. These pubs changed when the car-making industries moved away from the West Midlands and the smoking ban was introduced, creating venues that showcased Indian cuisine.

Today in West Bromwich, the same pubs that were once busy with manual workers now have crowds of football fans queuing up to buy pre-match pints and mixed grills. I've spoken to many British-Indians – who now attend football matches supporting West Brom – about the gruelling conditions in which their fathers worked, and the best link to that past is the desi pub.

This history, which goes back as far as post-war rationing, is remembered first-hand only by a few older regulars who still drink Mild, and not by many landlords. Apart from Suresh 'Suki' Patel who has been a publican at The Vine for 45 years and has seen a lot of social change.

His pub life encompasses all the themes I've mentioned in this book – from anti-racist resistance to culinary celebration – and he, more than anyone, is the reason why desi pub food has this smoked, BBQ culture. He made mixed grills popular in this area and his culinary influences show how the South Asian diaspora draws inspiration from places they come in contact with – places outside of India.

Patel is a 'twice migrant', a South Asian who came to the UK from a country outside South Asia – usually East and South Africa – who worked, or had ancestors that were employed, on plantations, railways and mines. In his case it was from Uganda, in 1967, when he was just a teenager. He was following his brother's path.

'The first day I came I wanted to go back,' admits Patel, though he realised if he was to make a life here, he would have to stick with it. His dad then followed in 1972, when Ugandan dictator Idi Amin told the Indian minority in the country to leave, causing more than 27,000 people to suddenly up sticks and move to the UK.

'My dad came empty handed when Amin chucked him out,' Patel says about his father who was an engineer at a sugar factory. 'He didn't have anything – he just came with his own clothes. He stayed with us.'

This sad episode of Indians in Africa does show how desi pub culture draws from many countries, regions and continents: Punjab, India, Nepal, Indo-China, Africa, and, of course, Britain.

'When I opened,' the 71-year-old tells me, 'all I had was the foundries. In those days it was hand pumps. I'd pull 30 or 40 pints and because they come from the foundries [at lunch] all they wanted was the first two pints. Never three.'

Patel is going to pass the pub on to his children. His son, Bharat, was born on the same day that he opened the pub. When I meet Bharat he's as jolly as his father, so the pub is in safe hands it seems.

When Patel started at the Vine, he was a tenant of Mitchells & Butlers, and there was no lager on offer, just mild, served at lunchtime until 2pm and from 7pm till closing. Today, mild can be found in a few pubs in Smethwick, but the biggest change to this pub isn't its drink range but how large it's become.

It used to be just three small rooms; the pub looked like a large semi-detached red-brick house. Now it's extended and very long and thin – think

Vine

Suresh 'Suki' Patel

Vine

of an ocean liner with a beer garden at the back, where the BBQ is located. (I say BBQ as it is more reminiscent of a large mangal in a Turkish restaurant.)

'I'm the first person to do BBQ,' he says. 'I was born in Africa and we used to do it on charcoal. One of my customers owned the factory [nearby] and they used to manufacture BBQs and he said "why don't you try?" I started it in the open air. People thought it was unique, especially with my home-made spice. The Sportsman [in West Brom] followed me, he was also a Patel. Now everywhere [you see] bar and grill!'

The spice used was a Guajarati masala and it was so popular that a big kitchen at the back had to be built to house the BBQ. 'Especially when white people came,' says Patel. 'Jesus, I had to build a temporary shed at the back!'

Today it's indoors and the centrepiece of a large dining room. It provides an excellent atmosphere, filling the building with gorgeous aromas and sizzling sounds.

'We have no more regulars,' says Patel. 'This generation doesn't want to play cards or dominoes – they look at their phones instead. In those days people would play and drink hard. Now it's all office jobs. People are not grafting like they used to.'

One of the favourite dishes today is chicken claypot, and, of course, the mixed grills, which punters happily watch being made on the BBQ.

'The Albion ground,' Patel says, 'is next door. We get all Albion fans – if it's a home game it's really busy. People come here have a few pints, BBQ, a few curries and go to the match and when the game is finished they come back.

'90% of people want spicy food. But they're still some people who want fish and chips – we do English food too. There's usually one in a group who doesn't like spicy food. This is a family pub – touch wood – I've been here 43 years, and I've not had any problems. Everyone comes with their wife and children.'

With the capacity to serve roughly 300 customers, the Vine is a big operation that employs about 25 staff members. 'If the game is a 3pm kick-off,' Patel says, 'they're here from 11am. Not all but gradually, and by 2pm we're rammed.'

The atmosphere on match days is different to other pubs based near a ground because West Brom is such an inclusive football club. Which is fitting because the Vine is a very diverse, welcoming institution. It might draw from African and Indian influences, but the Vine was always forward-looking and changed desi pub culture forever.

Suresh 'Suki' Patel

Vine

New Horseshoe Bar & Grill

1007 Foleshill Road, Coventry CV6 5HN
T 024 7666 6669
newhorseshoe.com
Mon–Thu 16.00–22.30; Fri–Sun 13.00–22.30.

Coventry has a long history of desi pubs stretching back to the 1960s when kabaddi teams would visit from all around the country and enjoy post-match pints at the Wheatsheaf on Foleshill Road. The beer garden at this traditional boozer would also feature a BBQ grill. The Wheatsheaf, therefore, has strong claims to be one of the country's first desi pubs, and is often spoken of fondly by the older generation.

Unfortunately, this history was interrupted when the Wheatsheaf stopped serving food and though it's still there – with kabaddi trophies and a new kitchen (called Star Grill producing Indian food for those on budget) – from the 1990s onwards desis would have to travel to nearby West Bromwich, Smethwick or Birmingham for mixed grills.

Then, in 2018 the New Horseshoe Bar & Grill opened, rejuvenating the city's desi pub culture by offering excellent food to a diverse base of customers. Nav Hayer runs the Horseshoe and the Hungry Elephant Bar & Grill (also in Coventry, but a bigger venue which opened more recently in between lockdowns) with his brother Jag, and they realised the winning formula after a stint owning the Shireland Bar & Grill in Smethwick.

'We were on a mission to bring desi pubs to Coventry,' he tells me. 'No one had done it well.'

Coventry isn't as diverse as other parts of the West Midlands, but it does have a sizeable non-white population with Asians accounting for 16.3% of the total. The Horseshoe is in the Foleshill district, which also houses an impressive Gurdwara (Sikh temple), and numerous working men's clubs, hinting at how brown and white live shoulder to shoulder.

'All my mum's side of the family,' Hayer says, 'they're from West Brom. So I was brought up in the desi pub culture going to the Vine, the Red Lion and the Sportsman. In Coventry there was more of a Bengali culture rather

than Punjabi desi. It was really only the Wheatsheaf in the mid 90s – they used to do BBQ. Straight. That's it. Eat it on a plastic plate. They started again about a year ago.'

The Horseshoe has 35% white customers while the Hungry Elephant has 85%. Both are really 'West Brom-style' desi pubs with, of course, mixed grills (and chips) as a large part of the offering. 'Everyone,' Hayer adds, 'who orders their food is going to have chips on the side. Is that just a Midlands thing? I don't know.'

We laugh and exchange stories of chips in (Midlands) desi pubs. The other feature – perhaps not by design – that aligns the Horseshoe to West Brom pubs is its close proximity to a football ground – in this case Coventry City (who are currently in the same league as West Brom.)

Despite being local rivals for promotion to the Premier League, traditionally Coventry cannot compete with WBA when it comes to desi pub match-day rituals. The ingrained post- and pre-match routine centring around mixed grills, curries and beers is much more nascent for many football fans in the West Bromwich area.

'We're getting busier,' says Man United supporter Nayer. 'And busier from the football side of things. I've experienced it growing up [at places like the Vine] but football fans [on match day] are coming here in this sort of environment and really liking it.

'And they're coming back and saying "This is the place to be after a game." We saw a gap in the market. When we had the Shireland, people were coming from Coventry to eat and we thought "why are they doing that?" We took a bit of a risk but and it is paying off at the moment.'

The hesitant 'at the moment' that bookended Nayer's sentence is probably due to the squeeze that he and his brother are feeling from rising prices and energy bills. Despite this, they still donate food as part of *sevadar* (the Sikh concept of community service). He used to have a regular job in IT, which, he recalled, would allow him to switch off at weekends. Now there's no such chance as hard graft is key to a pub's success.

'No one knows what will happen tomorrow,' he admits. 'You see it on the news about the shortages of tomatoes, lettuce and cucumber. We need them! Cooking onions have skyrocketed as well. Self-raising flour was £6 for 25kg in 2016. Now you're lucky if you can get it for less than £20.

'There's only so much you can put the prices up. There's only so much that you can keep absorbing. We're okay because we can bulk buy as we have two pubs, but fresh produce you can't bulk buy.'

Having two pubs means the menus (and ingredients) are almost identical, providing more bulk buying. Another plan is to buddy up with another desi pub landlord to increase their purchasing power, which shows how much initiative Nayer and his brother have. They must have inherited this (and his work ethic) from his dad who toiled in a foundry in Coventry and then had post-work pints in a pub.

'The new generation,' he says, 'would happily go out one evening every seven days. Before, everyone worked in a foundry and they needed that drink every day.'

Chicken balti

New Horseshoe Bar & Grill

If foundries were associated with the Midlands so are baltis and this was an ideal time to try one. I had it medium. I knew it would be spicy but plunged in, sweating like a tennis player during a five-set match at Wimbledon. It was worth persevering with, though. The chunks of chicken were large, moist and very tender, served with peppers that were crispy and sweet. The tarka dal I had was dense, with a nice cumin flavour throughout, and the garlic naan was perfect – one side soft, the other crunchy.

Just as I was leaving, Nayer's brother, Jag, reminded me to go to the Wheatsheaf, saying it was a bit different. And when I visited it was clear what he meant. It was more like a humble working men's club, with a desi kitchen in the backyard, almost as an afterthought.

Pubs like the Horseshoes put desi culture front and centre. As it always should be.

New Horseshoe Bar & Grill

Clockwise from top right: Chicken balti, dahl, garlic naan

Golden Lounge

59a Belgrave Road, Leicester LE4 6AS
T 0116 319 5505
thegoldenlounge.co.uk
Pub: *Mon, Wed & Thu 17.00–24.00; Fri & Saturday 17.00–02.00; Sun 17.00–23.00.*
Kitchen: *Mon, Wed & Thu 17.30–23.30; Fri & Sat 17.30–24.00; Sun 17.30–22.00.*

Leicester has one of the richest desi pub cultures in the country and can even boast (potentially) the first ever British-Indian pub, the Durham Ox, which was opened in 1962 by Sohan Singh. According to local newspapers, Singh had 'attractive English wife' (Janet, who helped him prepare Indian snacks), and had gained experience running his father's rum distillery in India.

'I must admit I'm a bit nervous,' he told Leicester's *Evening Mail* in 1962. 'Naturally, I'm aware of the responsibilities of the job. There will be a few difficult customers, no doubt, but I think I shall be able to manage.' The article concluded that Singh was chosen for the job because 'most of his customers were coloured people'. Sigh.

Fast forward 60 years and the Durham Ox still is a desi pub (although it's not run by the Singh family anymore and the owner, I'm told, is a Gujarati man who visits infrequently), and the area has many establishments I'd heartily recommend. Usually, I would pick one of these, detail its rich history, and explain how the publican (and customers) deal with a post-racism environment.

This is the approach I've adopted for this book, and because of that, it's been primarily a British story on how the Indian diaspora have changed the homogeneity of pubs while staying true to their roots.

The Golden Lounge, however, is a standout entry for those seeking an experience that's more Indian than British. It's an attempt to bring the contemporary food and music of the South Asian country to this island; and it's one that is 100% successful as security staff have to be employed to manage the queue at weekends.

The Golden Lounge is on Belgrave Road, on the inner edge of Leicester's Golden Mile, a road that became a hub for Asians fleeing Idi Amin's Ugandan

regime in 1972 after industry moved from the area making housing here affordable.

Unlike its equivalents in Manchester (Wilmslow Road's Curry Mile) and London (Brick Lane), this is not necessarily an area that white folk would consider heading for, despite it being famous for hosting what is claimed to be the largest Diwali celebration outside India.

But desis from all over the country visit and the Golden Lounge is now their focal point. I ventured here early in the day when it hadn't fully opened and the kitchen was being prepped. It was me and two other British-Asians supping lager. I told them about the book and they immediately understood why I was here and not at the Durham Ox: 'It's something different but excellent here,' one said. 'The food is really good,' the other chimed in.

The best way I can describe it is to compare it to the Prince of Wales in West Bromwich (p144), especially in the way the latter is like a bar that was shipped in from India. In the case of the PoW, it was an imagined establishment from when Jinder Birring Singh was a lot younger. But there's no retro feel here – this is a bar that feels like it was flown in yesterday.

The venture is relatively new; Shivam Sharma has been managing the Golden Lounge for only four or five months. Previously it was called the Golden Turmeric, and was more traditional, with sports vying for airtime with the other events.

Chicken lollipops

'The previous owner,' Sharma says, 'did music as well but the crowd was very different. They had older customers because they were playing 1980s and 1990s [Indian] music – now we have all ages.'

The music is performed on the weekends (Friday, Saturdays and Sundays) and the 'band' consists of the same two singers, who put in marathon shifts. Sharma says they will sing classic songs as well as new hits and it's dubbed 'karaoke' – most songs are done on a request basis with open mic one night a week. The Golden Lounge attracts people from all around the country – it's nearly 100% desis – because of this and they haven't needed to advertise once.

'It's mostly [British-] Indians,' Sharma says. 'We haven't done any marketing. Once we get the chance, we hope to publicise it, particularly the weekdays. Hopefully we're going to open another site based on an Indian village [bar].'

If it's getting a 100% British-Indian crowd you may be asking why I'm recommending this for a book that has wide appeal? The answer is two-fold: firstly, this could be interpreted as that dreaded word 'authentic'(see p24), which could see you gain an experience before other people realise a 'scene' is forming; secondly, the food is wonderful, and a genuine attempt to make the dining experience more Indian than British.

Yes there are mixed grills but there's also an egg equivalent served on a platter (masala eggs sizzler) and egg Angara masala – boiled eggs cooked in a spicy gravy. 'I love eggs,' Sharma says. 'Gujarat cooks can make 150–200 dishes from eggs. The masala eggs sizzler is most like this style of cooking.'

Sadly, I'm intolerant to eggs, so I plump for chicken lollipops, which Sharma also says is one of his favourites. I'm sceptical because he seems to be enthused about so many dishes on his menu, but when I taste the chicken, I know he's telling the truth.

The skin is crispy, the smell of the spices is incredible, the meat is tender and there's a secondary fire from the Szechuan spice – surprising as Indo-Chinese dishes are normally on the milder side. The dhal makhana is super rich and goes so well with my bullet naan (filled with green chilies) that I ended up ordering a second portion of the bread cooked on the tandoor.

The attempt at creating food, especially the curries, just like it tastes in India leads to a startling announcement from Sharma. Because of the hardness and fluoride added to British water, Sharma claims that our food – especially stews (like curries) and dhals – tastes different.

'I struggled to drink the water when I came here,' he says. 'I just wasn't used to it. When we get really busy we will try to bring the water from India.'

There would be logistical issues to this, but if you can bring an entire bar from India and give people a slice of modern South Asian life then who's going to stop Sharma? Whatever the case, the Golden Lounge is worth travelling for, whatever part of the country you're based in. Even though the car or train ride might take a long time, it's a lot quicker than a flight to India.

Dhal makhana

Golden Lounge

Tap & Tandoor

53 Cumbergate, Queensgate Shopping Centre, Peterborough PE1 1YR
T 01733 312444
tapandtandoor.co.uk
Mon 16.00–24.00; Tue–Sun 12.00–24.00.

With nearly 15% of the population identifying as Asian, Peterborough is a prime spot for a successful desi pub. What I wasn't expecting was this much-needed British-Indian boozer, an outpost of Solihull's Tap & Tandoor (p133), to be nestled amongst an ornate 17th-century English restoration guildhall and metres away from the city's cathedral.

But why shouldn't this be a fitting place for a desi pub? The formula has been honed successfully in the Midlands by publican Ajay Kenth and he even pitches it as a 'gastropub' serving fine food and craft beers. You would expect an Italian here with outside dining – in fact the building used to be a Carluccio's – so why not somewhere offering excellent meals and drinks?

I guess it's hard to recalibrate our minds because when you're used to going to parts of North London and the Midlands for Indian food in a pub setting, it becomes a new experience to visit a cathedral city and experience desi dining at its best.

Although this is now a mini-chain (another T&T has opened in Southampton just before this book was published), the ingredients (and beers) are often sourced locally. This means that the area's excellent produce – and local breweries – can be tapped into.

I start with chili chicken, which has the usual Indo-Chinese spicing (but feels fresher) and large chunks of moist breast – in fact, it's inner fillet. 'It's like when you have chicken tenders in a fried chicken shop. So it's a little bit softer,' Kenth tells me afterwards.

I found this perfectly paired with SALT Brewery's Jute, a very sessionable IPA with citrus tones and a sharp but light flavour. Drinking paler ales with spicy food, rather than lagers, is something that was recommended when I visited the Crafty Indian in Shipley (p168), close to where Salt is brewed, and Kenth agrees with this approach.

SALT Jute

Tap & Tandoor

Fish curry

Chili chicken

'The hoppier the beer then the better it will go with the food,' says Kenth. '[With these beers] the palate feel is a lot better and with spicy food it works really well.'

I find the food here very indulgent and the aptly named 'special naan' is very rewarding as it contains cheese, chili and garlic. It's hard to talk about naan breads without avoiding the word 'pillow-y' but it tears apart softly and is perfect with my fish curry (the sauce is excellent, very tomato-y and a perfect foil for the fresh mustard seeds and curry leaves).

The T&T works really well here in Peterborough. There's an established craft beer savvy market as well as a lot of bar hoppers, particularly on a Friday and Saturday night. There's also a Punjabi community who previously travelled to Leicester for their desi pub kicks but now have a great pub to call their local. That's exactly what the T&T does well. It could shun the casual drinker who's apprehensive about craft but really prides itself in offering a desi welcome to all.

'Ultimately, we're in hospitality,' concludes Kenth. 'So it's about being hospitable. You've got to have conversations with your customers to find out what they want.'

It shows that steering a customer to a craft beer is similar to educating them as to what curry they should order to match their heat tolerance. It sounds simple but here it's done very well and on a midweek day there are plenty of drinkers as well as happy diners showing the Tap is equal to the Tandoor.

Tap & Tandoor

North of England & Scotland

Crafty Indian

34–38 Bradford Road, Shipley BD18 3NT
T 01274 588114
thecraftyindian.com
Tue–Fri 17.00–22.00; Sat & Sun 17.00–22.00.

Despite fostering inclusion, serving quality Indian food, and working hard for their community, desi pub landlords are sometimes criticised for not putting a lot of thought into their beer selection. When you weigh up that one charge against all the positives it really does seem like a petty criticism to level at a type of publican that does so much for wider society.

There are obvious exceptions to this general rule: the Glad in South London (p68), the Regency and Tamil Prince in North London (p44 and 56), and the Indian Brewery (p104) and Tap & Tandoor chain (p160, p164, p185) But that's not a lot of instances where British-Indians have embraced craft beer and looked beyond multinationals, such as Cobra and Kingfisher.

I discuss why this is in detail in the introduction (p29), but I feel that maybe a generational shift is taking place as more desi pubs turn 'gastro', innovate, and are taken over by younger publicans. Presently, though, that marks anyone who does look to serve beers that may need a little explaining – such as New England IPAs and German Pilsners – as outliers.

It helps if you're located in a place that has a strong craft tradition with a lot of local breweries that produce interesting, innovative beer. Shipley is one such area. It's next door to Saltaire, which houses SALT Beer Factory, and is near to Leeds, Manchester and Sheffield.

It's also a factor if the owner is driven to offer something more ethical. Harry Khinda at the Crafty Indian is passionate about sustainability and even offers reusable tiffin tins for his customers ordering takeaway, which is a world away from a lot of 'street food-style' outlets that use disposable cutlery and plates to give a market feel (and to save time and labour by avoiding washing up).

'Our business is partly based on sustainability,' he tells me on the phone (he's unable to meet during my visit as he's sustained a back injury). 'We like to use metal plates, they go into the wash and last for ages. Some

street food places use degradable plates, etc., but it still goes into landfill and I don't see the sense in that.'

What's all the more surprising is that the Crafty Indian was a traditional Indian curry house – Zaara's – run by Khinda. He's been in this spot for 16 years, but admits, 'It wasn't working. I wasn't enjoying it.'

Although Khinda is in a lot of pain when we speak, he's happy to hear that I really enjoyed the beer I was served with my meal. It was Schneider's Bayrish Hell, a helles (which is often interpreted to be pale or light) with a light carbonation and which complemented my meal well due to its light fruit (apple-y) flavours. This cheered Khinda up because, like me, he's no fan of brands, such as Cobra.

'I don't even think lager is the best drink to have with Indian food,' he says. 'Pale ales using a huge raft of different fruits and flavour profiles complemented with the spices from the food just make eating an Indian meal so much more pleasurable. Especially when you have a range of different profiles in your beer.

'It's similar to when you have European food and you choose red meat paired with red wine. Otherwise, the idea of going for a curry is having 10 pints of lager and a vindaloo, and then who cares what the curry tastes like?

'But when you have different profiles of craft beer you can definitely bring out different flavours in the food by pairing it with the right beer.'

Despite not believing that lager is the best pairing for Indian food, Khinda believes that it can work with lagers that aren't necessarily 'craft'; for example, German beers that are brewed by big companies (to strict purity laws).

'We use a lot of German lagers that are relatively unknown in this country. You won't find them everywhere because they are a lot more expensive – like Dortmunder beer. I'll be surprised if you can find a better tasting lager.'

He does admit that the German lager is only used over British brands

Pani puri

Dhaba chicken

because of its quality, but where possible, Khinda looks closer to home. 'Why serve Foster's when you have microbreweries on your doorstep?' he asks.

The food that he serves also bucks a trend from a lot of desi pubs in that the heat is not at high levels. At first I thought that was because he was catering to a mainly white crowd, but it turns out it's because Khinda believes that's what Indian food should be like.

'It's a myth that a chicken vindaloo or whatever burns your head off. It's not meant to do that,' he says.

Instead, the dishes that arrive at our table are more delicately balanced. I order pani puri, which is a favourite snack of mine but rarely found on my travels even though it's perfect with beer. And unlike ones I've had before, they come apart easily – 'like Kinder eggs,' my dining companion says – and allow the tamarind to be filled inside the half dome. Unlike the favourite Italian kids' treat, these are a flavour sensation, and served this way offer none of the mess of a normal pani puri, which have to be eaten whole.

The Thali – an Indian platter – comes with a mutton curry that is very tender, and garlic chili chicken, fried chicken with an array of spices. The Aloo tikka chaat offers a nice punctuation to the meat dishes, while the standout dish is the keema, which has the oil on top – often this is spooned off for aesthetic purposes, though makes little sense as we eat the oil in a chunky lamb curry. The dhaba chicken and garlic coriander naan were also superb, the sauce soothing and the bread fresh and soft.

The whole experience showed how superior the dining experience can be when you add craft (and German) beer into the mix. Hopefully, this is a taste of things to come as more and more desi pubs and bar owners realise the potential of keeping the beer micro. Thinking small (and local) might make their businesses bigger after all.

Crafty Indian

Peacock Bar

25 North Parade, Bradford BD1 3JL
T 07863 863163
peacockbar.co.uk
Mon 16.00–22.00; Tue 15.00–22.30; Wed 15.00–24.00; Thu 15.00–22.30;
Fri & Sat 12.00–01.00; Sun 13.00–23.00. (Call ahead if planning to come early).

When people ask me to name my favourite desi pub I often bat the question back to them. I do this to work out what criteria they use and often they're looking for where I've had the best meal. This is, in itself, very difficult to answer as how a food tastes can depend on so many factors, including the mood you're in at the time.

Although food is an important factor, it's only one of the many ways I judge a desi pub's quality. The main one I use – which works for all pubs – is 'community', because it shows that you will be treated warmly, and, as a valued customer, you are contributing to a vital support network. This setup requires a publican who treats his customers like an extended family, cares deeply about their plight, and contributes a great deal to good causes.

In many ways this shows how deeply unfair British society is. During the pandemic supermarket profits increased substantially and hospitality suffered because all types of food and drink had to be bought from these retailers. Then, when inflation and rising energy prices led to cost increases, these same huge chains – with shareholders raking in profits – got you and me to absorb the difference.

To make matters worse, alcohol sold in these stores isn't subject to the same levels of taxation as in pubs. This means that responsible drinking, with a landlord overseeing consumption, is a lot more expensive for the customer and less profitable for pubs.

We also tacitly accept that a supermarket isn't the place you go to if you need companionship – the very thought of this even seems perverse. In fact, I recently witnessed a shop assistant being reprimanded by his manager for talking to an old woman instead of stacking shelves.

It's easy to make assumptions that community support in pubs only happens in certain areas of the country. But a good desi pub, regardless of

Some of the Peacock's regulars

its location, will have customers who all know each other, and a landlord who helps instigates this warm belonging. When I was walking around Bradford in the snow, peering into a few bars selling cheap cocktails and shots, I feared the opposite. I thought the pub I had chosen to visit would be a high street bar with a transient crowd – the kind of place you could visit for years and not have one meaningful interaction.

At the Peacock Bar, however, I found the opposite. This was in many ways my ideal desi pub with a very mixed crowd – 50/50 desi and white – with food served on an ad hoc basis, and decent, affordable drinks. Its community focus was so strong that I felt moved hearing about the football team it sponsors, the free curry given out during carol services, and how it was used as a church on Sundays. Hindu owners helping Christians.

I guess it's in Mithun Mistry's DNA. His father opened Bharat, a club and restaurant in the city which people would travel around the country to visit for special occasions (they even have one of the original beer pumps displaying its installation date in 1984). The family business is so successful they have two other outlets – one selling craft and another Peacock in Bingley, which Mistry admits is more food orientated.

Here, the most popular dish is spam pakoras. Mistry, maybe tongue-in-cheek, says spam is really popular in Bradford because of the boar (he's even named his craft bar the Boar & Fable), which is a historic symbol of the city and can be found in many statues and emblems near old buildings. Maybe there's some truth in this as the local chippies serve spam fritters. In any case, the spam pakoras are delicious, like spicy cholesterol cigars, and perfect with my beer.

And that's not the only unique item that Mistry cooks. He proudly tells me about his chicken liver curry (all the ingredients are bought from the nearby indoor market). 'It's the cheapest part of the chicken,' he says. 'The liver is quite big though. They were really popular in my dad's club. It's the opposite of slow cooking. If anything you have to make sure you don't overcook it.'

There's also naan-bread pizza (perfect as the base is softer than its Italian cousin), spiced lamb chops, and the kind of fare you'd expect, such as marinated meats and curries. All this is perfect grazing food while you're drinking and it's no surprise that Mistry's meals go down well at festivals. The menu may be ad hoc at the moment because Mistry normally works the kitchen, with dedicated bar staff in situ, but today he's running between the stove and the pumps, as well as answering my questions.

Pint of cask Tetley's

Peacock Bar

Spam pakora

'When you come next time we'll have a full menu,' he says breathlessly.

I can't wait for next time because my visit was so soothing. I could even tick a wish off my beer bucket list – having a pint of Tetley's on a hand-pulled cask. This was smooth, with a lovely head and possibly the most sessionable bitter I've ever tasted. Mistry says it was always on at Bharat and loved by the older desis, and I can see why. Now it's a guest beer and not a regular, so my luck was in. I can see why it's a pub popular with CAMRA members, who recognise a good pint when they see it.

I chat to the locals and discover several of them have moved to Bradford from the south, which reminds me of a similar community pub a long way away – The Ypres Castle in Rye, where the regulars have bonded by being new arrivals to the town. I imagine this is why I've been treated like a local when I've visited there – and here, too.

All this makes me want to recommend this pub to all types of people. I even think it's worth the trip from wherever you live. It may be snowing outside, but this is the warmest place in the country.

Peacock Bar

Sheepscar Bar & Grill

Savile Drive, Leeds LS7 3EJ
T 0113 262 3086
thesheepscarbarandgrill.co.uk
Mon–Thu 17.00–22.00; Fri 17.00–22.30; Sat 13.00–22.30; Sun 13.00–22.00.

Most of the areas featured in this book are very new to me, so I approach them from the perspective of a tourist, albeit one with a lot of knowledge recently acquired about desi pub culture. In the case of Leeds, it's both familiar and distant because I lived there in the 1990s when I first left home (though haven't returned since).

Brain experts believe that this period – when you first become an adult and gain some freedom – is when the songs you listen to are the tunes you return to the most as you grow older. I also think that your food, beer and leisure tastes, as well as musical preferences, are formed in this period of nascent maturity. When I lived here there was an Indian restaurant at the end of my road where you could bring in massive jugs of beer from the next-door pub. The curry house (the Corner Café, one of the first in Leeds) only shuttered recently and the neighbouring boozer is now a Tesco Express.

My love of beer and curry must have come from this sadly fading part of the city, but there was no desi pub culture in the area that I could tap into. If I had stayed living there, though, I would have had the Sheepscar Bar and Grill, which opened 15 years ago on the site of a working men's club in the Meanwood/Chapeltown area of the West Yorkshire city.

It's a bit more than a pub. It's actually a huge, multi-purpose venue that has an area that can be hired for celebrations. These are culturally important to desis, particularly those of Punjabi origin, as they gave them a chance to celebrate occasions other than weddings, leading to women being more involved in drinking and pub culture.

When I visit the Sheepscar it's a bleak, icy day of sleet and the threat of heavy snow. From the road the building looks like a large industrial unit but when you approach it's obvious that it's something special. I'm not the

only one to feel discombobulated by the Sheepscar experience. Inside a guy who, like me, used to live in Leeds says he's passed this pub many times but has never ventured inside. 'I can't believe it,' he says.

Neither of us were expecting the impressive decor, modern furnishings, and the striking, bright, custard baize of the pool tables. I could describe the interior as modern but that would be doing it a disservice – it's more like sci-fi or something from the dark TV series *Black Mirror*, especially with the many prominent screens.

The mixed grill – apparently, it's won awards for being the best in Yorkshire – was very good. The fish pakora had a very light batter with succulent fish pieces; the deliciously charred wings were sat at the bottom on the grill so they soaked up the browned onions and lemon juice; the lamb pieces were tender but hot and spicy; while the lamb chops were small but super succulent. The kofte was a bit disappointing, but in my opinion they're never the best part of a mixxy, maybe because they seem insulated from the onions, lemon and charring.

The Sheepscar is extremely busy most days and I recommend booking, especially if you're visiting on the off chance like I did. It's a desi pub that makes me feel slightly sad because I wish I had this kind of option when I was becoming an adult in Leeds.

But having a mixed grill on a cold day made me feel like that young man who once thought he knew everything, especially about food. Considering how I misjudged what to expect from the exterior, it shows we're both still learning.

Soho Tavern

Front Street, Kibblesworth, Gateshead NE11 0YJ
T 191 697 4432
sohotavern.co.uk
Mon–Sun 12.00–23.00.

Branching out to a new area for desi pub landlords must be hugely daunting, especially if it's a village setting. The countryside has been a hostile place to people of colour; I grew up in a semi-rural Bedfordshire market town 30-odd years ago and my childhood, as I've mentioned, was scarred by prejudice. But it's vital for British-Indians to prosper if desi pubs can open in settings where there is little representation of empowered community figures – and there's none more so than a pub landlord.

It takes someone with a lot of energy to explain the concept of a desi pub and how it differs from a curry house, takeaway and a traditional pub to those unfamiliar. As my visit to Glasgow's Glassy Central (p181) shows, this might not be enough if the locals don't consider you as a place for drinks and think the food should compete with budget takeaways where it's price first and quality second.

Kibblesworth is a former mining village, a community that was entirely based around the pit and brickworks until it closed in 1974. It's clearly modernised since those days, but you can still see the old electrical lines that were for a tram system, while its pub was definitely the beating heart of the village.

To come here and plonk a desi pub right in the centre of the village takes courage, but when The Plough was put up for sale, Johnny Singh, brother of Mikey (see p116) didn't see it as a challenge. Instead, it was an opportunity for the Soho Tavern to branch out from the Midlands – they have one in Birmingham and another in West Bromwich – into a new untapped market.

'It was an English village pub,' he says. 'They did standard traditional Sunday dinners. Over a 10-year period they had a new manager every year. They ran it as a wet pub with Sunday lunch and toasties.'

'It was a massive [financial] investment. It had sticky carpets, church-like benches and it was very cold. It was empty – sometimes there would be 10 people visiting all day. But I wasn't nervous opening here. Nowadays I recommend people book at the weekends.'

Singh's success was to make the pub a destination, with people travelling from as far north as Glasgow and from places to the south, such as Leeds and Bradford.

'We cook fresh,' he says. 'Fresh spices, full of flavour. People have never had that here. They're used to curry house food, with added sugar and colourings. We have spice levels where you can go from mild to hot. Everything is tailored for people's needs.'

The option here to build your own curries with whatever meat, veg or fish you want coupled with different bases and altered spice levels is a hugely successful – and easily comprehensible – import from the Soho Tavern. The staff are trained by Singh to explain how this works and to empower customers to add ingredients and spices so that the dish is suited to their personal tastes and heat tolerance.

I put this to the test by ordering a chicken tikka with saag (spinach) with a medium heat level. The dish comes with beautifully marinated chicken pieces that contrast hugely with the green vegetable base. It looks like it should be a mild dish because of this but it's fairly fiery. I can take a lot of heat normally but I think the step up from this to 'spicy' would have been too much and would have overpowered the subtle flavours.

'It was a big surprise,' Singh admits. 'A lot of people who come here like it hot and they say they can tolerate heat so I point them to our chicken Punjabi curry.'

One of the most surprising aspects of this is that nearby Newcastle, despite being a diverse dining and drinking hotspot, has nothing like the Soho Tavern. There are curry houses and decent pubs but no place caters for a customer who wants spice and quality ingredients all washed down with pints of beer. When I tell my friends who live in Newcastle about the Soho Tavern they immediately say 'we're going!' and I know they won't be disappointed.

The Soho Tavern works well here because its brand fits the northeast's gastro scene, which is, basically, a highfalutin'

Johnny Singh

Soho Tavern

way of saying 'they love chips.' But this isn't something to trivialise. As mentioned in the Birmingham entry (p116), the most popular dish is chili chips, and the same goes here. But there's a twist.

'Cheesy chips are very common in the northeast,' says Johnny, 'but once they try our chili cheese chips they go "oh my, God. This is unbelievable. What is this?"'

I put them to the test. The crispy texture of the chili sauce-infused chips (they won't reveal their secret) is made even more indulgent by the melted cheese. It still remains a huge mystery how the chips can remain so firm despite a thick duvet of mozzarella covering them. I'd be lying if I said they weren't filling, and this is perhaps the nearest I've come to having a 'pizza' in a desi pub (apart from at the Peacock in Bradford, p171), albeit one with a deep fried potato 'base'.

Maybe because people are travelling from around Britain to come here, there is a notable desi presence among the customers, which shows how much of a success the pub is by drawing in such a diverse crowd.

'There's an Asian community in Newcastle,' says Singh. 'It's not like Birmingham's but you notice it more when this place opened. A lot of Punjabis came. For the [white] English community it was very new for them but once they tried the food, they loved it.

Soho Tavern

'Once they come in they smell the ginger and coriander. You go to a normal curry house and you can't smell that. It's all cooked fresh when they order.'

He's right. Because of the amount of travelling people do – particularly football fans, who are the most likely to venture to the Midlands for a pre-match mixed grill – the standards of desi pub food are so high that everything has to be a lot fresher than in a curry house, known for using pre-cooked sauces.

This is another element of the Soho Tavern's success in Gateshead: match days. Newcastle has always been a football-mad city, and these days the team is riding high with new Saudi owners bankrolling them. The Soho Tavern has tapped into this wave of fandom by offering supporters a quality food and drink option before and after games. They're also packed when Newcastle matches are televised live.

Newcastle United aren't yet title challengers as they look to build the right team, but the Soho Tavern has a winning formula – one that produces results every time a customer visits.

Chicken tikka with saag

Cheesy chips

Soho Tavern

Glassy Central

285 Sauchiehall Street, Glasgow G2 3HQ
T 0141 332 7565
Mon–Fri 16.00–24.00; Sat 12.00–24.00; Sun 16.00–24.00.

Glasgow and its surrounding area has by far the largest community of British Asians in Scotland, so you would think that it would have a rich history of desi pubs, especially with its legacy of heavy industry. Sadly, the opposite is true.

It does have a sizable Punjabi population, which would suggest that in the past there was a clamour for drinking establishments, as in parts of London and the Black Country, and a supply of desi landlords ready to pull pints. But in many ways, Glasgow explains why some areas have large populations of the Indian diaspora integrated into the local community but no desi pubs. Despite the city's rich curry house tradition, desis never set up their own pubs, according to Kinder Singh, because they didn't take jobs that led to a culture of having pints after work.

Another reason is that families of Punjabi origin now find themselves scattered across the city after initially being based in the western parts when they first started arriving from the 1960s. They also worked hours that were not conducive to pub-going, in jobs that demanded anti-social work patterns, such as working at weekends.

Singh's dad ran a shop in Finnieston (just west of the city centre) in the 1980s and his father's experience, he believes, reflects the day-to-day life of many Punjabis who came to Scotland's largest city. 'Near our house was a pub called Bannister's,' he tells me. 'My dad's routine after closing the shop was to go there, have two pints, come home, have two shots of whisky, tarka dal, roti, sleep.'

He would have loved to have Indian food in the pub in those days, like the ones that were set up in West Brom or London, but that wasn't the case. Instead, the only spicy food being cooked on the high street was at the city's many curry houses.

'Originally,' Singh says, 'it was the Bengalis who had the restaurants up here. Then the Indians came in.'

The Bengalis, Singh mentions, ran the first Bangladeshi curry houses cooking the 'Indian' food we're all familiar with: huge menus ranging from kormas to vindaloos, with poppadoms and shish kebabs all churned out at cheap prices. These were businesses run for both lunchtime diners and the post-pub crowd – open from noon till two in the morning –serving pints when Britain's licensing laws shut boozers early.

One good example of this kind of restaurant was the Koh-I-Noor, opened in 1964, where most Glaswegians had their first curries, including famous residents such as Billy Connolly and Lulu.

When the clamour for Indian food similar to the quality of other cities such as Birmingham and London, became overwhelming, the Bangladeshis moved further north in Scotland, according to Singh, and Indians started to take over their restaurants.

But this meant the city's diners (and drinkers) had no idea about desi pubs, and, crucially, their evolution from wet pubs to Indian fine dining (yes, I'm using that term because I sincerely believe they are a world away from a Bangladeshi-run curry house). Because of this, it takes a lot of explaining about how desi pubs are as much an alternative to a traditional boozer as any restaurant.

Singh didn't have a brand to lean on – like the Soho Tavern's Gateshead outpost – when he opened his establishment in 2021, but his enthusiasm for desi pubs was so great he named it Glassy Central, after the legendary Glassy Junction in Southall, West London.

'Whenever I was in London,' Singh says, 'I would always go to the Scotsman (p75) and the Glassy. When we first opened we even started doing the jumbo naans like in the Scotsman.'

Kinder Si

The heavy lifting of explaining how a 'Punjabi' desi pub is different to a restaurant was so demanding that he ended up compromising, calling it an 'Indian restaurant' so that a wider audience would know what to expect. There wasn't a big enough market of Punjabi desis – although people did travel from far and wide – and white customers hadn't grown accustomed to the culture.

'We still get Punjabis,' he says. 'But it's fluctuating. In the city centre [where Glassy is based] I think they come and go. For it to be busy all the time will take another year.

Glassy Central

'I had a restaurant before this and I used to get 15–20 Asian families regular dine there and this is why I thought it was the time to open this pub.'

Despite the branding saying otherwise, this is still a pub, which even occupies a space that used to be an Irish boozer (although it was an Italian restaurant before that). It's not at street level so it does feel like you're walking into a basement diner, but once you see the bar, the TV screens playing sports, and Singh's warm welcome it's clear that this place is very different to a curry house.

In fact, the food is so good I'd say it marries the best parts of a curry house with a desi pub kitchen: reasonable priced, home-style cooking in a community setting and a landlord who is curious about your day. Currently, Singh is undercharging his customers and admits the prices will have to rise – charging £10 for a mixed grill, made with quality ingredients, that can be shared by two in a city centre setting is not viable. Soon this will rise by at least £5, which is still very affordable.

To start off I had 'desi' chicken wings, which were fiery and blackened on the tandoor. These had a crispy, charred skin with a nice moist flesh – perfect for sharing and a great starter to a meal (and conversations). Singh wanted me to taste his pakoras, which were cooked fresh for me and were possibly the least greasy ones I've ever eaten.

To round things off I went against one of my own desi pub 'rules' and ordered a rice dish. It takes a special occasion for me to break the code and risk being bloated, but, like a lot of people of Indian descent, I have a soft spot for biryani as it was cooked for memorable moments.

Glassy Central

Vegan biryani

Glassy's biryani didn't disappoint. I went for a vegan version with soya chunks and Singh upped the heat levels to 'desi' hot. For a rice dish, it's hellishly addictive and reminded me of how my mum made hers (it's as close as I've come on my travels to a 'mom 'n' pop'-type desi kitchen which is able to produce dishes that are homely).

'This street used to have four or five Indian restaurants', says Singh. 'Now I'm the only one.'

'But Glaswegians can eat spicy food and they want decent dishes. You've got to take pride in what you cook and you've got to be proud to say "that curry's mine". I want the chef to make a curry with their heart and not just for the pay packet at the end of the week.'

This pub will be thriving in the future as the authorities in Glasgow look to make Sauchiehall Street a 'strip' with just bars, pubs and restaurants. Singh admits it would make sense from a policing point of view and would give the famous old street a new focus as a hedonistic hub for food and drink lovers.

Desi chicken wings

As I'm leaving a man comes in for a takeaway and orders a beer. He sits down quietly, and I wonder how much happier he would be if he realised that there's more fun in dining out than sitting at home. It might be discombobulating for him to see the Punjabi TV channels, the noises from the kitchen and the sizzling platters suddenly being brought into a bar area, but for me this is when I'm happiest.

Glassy Central might be confusing to some but it really is simple: drink beer, order food, and be treated like royalty by Singh.

Best of the Rest

LONDON

Everest Spice (The Honeypot)

178 Honeypot Lane, Stanmore, Middlesex HA7 3BU · T 0208 206 1024 · everesthoneypot.com
Mon–Thu 12.00–15.00, 18.00–23.00; Fri & Sat 12.00–15.00, 18.00–24.00; Sun 12.00–23.00.

This is the place to visit if you want to see a big football match on TV while enjoying Indian food. The Everest also has an outpost in Stanmore 'village', the **Everest Abercorn**, which is another large (country-style) boozer that has been turned desi. In the case of The Honeypot, it gained a tradition for excellent Indian food when it was run by Kalpesh Amlani (Purple Flame, p40) from 2005 to 2012. Now there's a Nepalese slant, so as well as the usual sizzling suspects, it has a vast range of vegetarian dishes, including a Haweli kofta curry – a dumpling cooked in spinach sauce.

Park View

156 Bowes Road, Arnos Grove, London N11 2JG · T 0208 881 1575 · parkviewclub.com
Tue–Thu 17.00–23.00; Fri & Sat 17.00–24.00; Sun 17.00–23.00.

Being a big fan of desi pub/clubs of North London, I couldn't not mention Park View, which offers great south Asian food in a relaxed environment (and it's common not to be ushered away outside of the advertised hours). This is a more chilled, less restaurant-y version of the Tamil Prince (p56), with Sri Lankans offering different dishes (although there's still Indian fare, such as desi lamb), such as Mari Egg, which comes in a black pepper and ginger garlic paste, and a mutton roll. You'll have to trust me about this one as it looks unassuming (like a shop) from the outside, but it's really worth coming out of your comfort zone for.

Terrace

96–100 High Street, Southall UB1 3DN · T 0208 574 3335 · theterracesouthall.com
Sun–Thu 12.00–23.00; Fri & Sat 12.00–24.00.

Southall has needed a desi pub that's 'modern' for a few years now because the Scotsman (p75) and Prince of Wales aren't set up for family dining, if, like me, you have young kids. What the area has also required is a pub that has been revamped like the ones found in the Midlands. Based where the Red Lion used to be located, this is a great addition to London's desi pub scene with rooftop dining and specials, such as a huge leg of lamb that comes with naan breads. I highly recommend visiting here, having a paan leaf, and then heading over to the Scotsman for a nightcap.

SOUTH OF ENGLAND

Tap & Tandoor

Westquay Shopping Centre, Southampton SO15 1DE · T 023 8063 8852
southampton@tapandtandoor.co.uk · *Mon–Thu 12.00–23.00 (kitchen closes 21.15);*
Fri & Sat 12.00–24.00 (kitchen closes 21.30); Sun 12.00–22.00 (kitchen closes 21.15).

The Tap & Tandoor 'gastro' mini-chain, which includes Peterborough (p164) and Solihull (p133), recently opened this Southampton branch as this book was being published. The key to its success is to include local beers so that residents who aren't au fait with a desi pub understand that it's not just about the food. Here they can have a pint of Vibrant Forest Brewery Pupa (a juicy, sessionable, American-style IPA) with their okra fries. Being in the food quarter means it's likely to have more diners than drinkers, but there is a sizable desi population in Southampton. This isn't the city's first British-Indian pub; **Five Rivers** offers a more traditional sports atmosphere.

Tap & Tandoor

MIDLANDS

Merrymaid Bar & Grill

263 Moseley Road, Highgate, Birmingham B12 0EA
T 0121 440 3043 · Sun–Thu 12.00–23.00; Fri & Sat 12.00–24.00.

The decor here is unassuming but the atmosphere is warm, and the food is terrific. The mixed grills are renowned for being the best value in the country. This is the place you need to visit if you're after no-frills dining and to view what desi pubs were like before they became revamped to court families and people visiting from other areas. It's simple and it should be shared – this is ideal for large groups who want sizzling platters and plenty of beer. If you're looking for a dining experience that doesn't have paper tablecloths, try the equally excellent **Covered Wagon** (thecoveredwagon.co.uk), two miles away in Moseley.

Champy's Bradford Arms

504 Pleck Road, Walsall WS2 9HE · T 01922 641439 · champys.co.uk
Pub: Mon–Fri 16.00–23.00; Sat & Sun 13.00–23.00.
Kitchen: Mon–Fri 16.00–22.00; Sat & Sun 14.00–22.00.

Also a world away from the Merrymaid is the oddly named Champy's, in a totally revamped, family-friendly, relaxed establishment. It turns out the pub was named after a local, AKA John or Champy, who kindly built a BBQ room after a fire in the 1990s sparked by a broken paraffin heater. The most recent chef is from Nepal and he has experimented with a range of dishes, much to the locals' appreciation. The sweetcorn fritters, crispy wings and chicken tikka in tamarind sauce are highly recommended, and the kids will love their chicken korma and rice (£6).

Champy's Bradford Arms

Sportsman Bar & Restaurant

13/15 High Street, West Bromwich B70 6PP · T 0121 553 1353
sportsmanbarandrestaurant.co.uk · Pub: *Mon–Sun 12.00–23.00.* Kitchen: *Mon–Sun 12.00–22.30.*

The Sportsman was one of the first pubs in the Midlands to have a BBQ grill
after it saw the popularity of Suki Patel's at The Vine (p152). Interestingly,
the owner then (in the 1990s) was a Singh (Punjabi origin) but now they
have owners of Gujarati heritage, like Patel. It shows how a Punjabi grill
was actually of Indian-African origin. Its other claim to fame was that it was
reviewed in *The Guardian* by restaurant critic Jay Rayner, who enthused about
its various marinated meats. It's recently been refurbed and it's a great desi
pub all-rounder – perfect for watching sport, casual dining or just having a
few beers. On the few times I've visited I've found the locals really friendly,
especially if you 'let' them win at pool as I have.

Sportsman Bar & Restaurant

Glassy Junction

131 Willenhall Road, Wolverhampton WBV1 2HR · T 01902 454040 · ojbasra@hotmail.com
Sun–Thu 12.00–23.00; Fri & Sat 12.00–24.00.

Named after the legendary boozer in Southall (now a vegetarian restaurant),
this functional looking pub (with an events area) offers a great mixed grill
and other hot dishes. Onkar Basra – who is a friend of Jinder at the Prince of
Wales (p144) – runs a great pub with people travelling from all around the

Glassy Junction

Midlands for the sizzling dishes and rich curries. One chef is from the Punjab, one from Mumbai, and the other from North India, and because of this the food has lots of influences but still fully grounded in British desi pub culture as the hugely popular, and tasty, mixed grill shows.

Paddy's Marten Inn

98 Martin Street, Leicester LE4 6EU · T 0116 266 5123 · paddysmarteninn.co.uk
Tue–Sun 17.00–22.00.

When I decided to cover the Golden Lounge (p160) for the Leicester section I did so because it offered something different to all the other pubs in the city – as well as all the other places I've visited in the country. Leicester does have a thriving desi pub scene and Paddy's is a good first option if you're looking for a similar experience to a bar and grill in West Brom or Smethwick: that is, quality curries and sizzlers served in a traditional pub. The Mashrus took over this former Irish pub in the mid 1990s after running a busy café in Loughborough bus station. Other options in the city include **Blue Peter** on Law Street and the **Woolpack** (woolpackleicester.com)

About the author

DAVID JESUDASON is a British-Asian journalist who specialises in food, drink and cultural history. He writes for newspapers and magazines around the world, including *BBC Culture*, *The Guardian*, *Wired*, *Huff Post*, *Atlas Obscura* and *Good Beer Hunting*. In 2022 he won the British Guild of Beer Writers' awards for Best Communication about Diversity in Beer and Pubs, and Best Comissioned Beer Writing. He was also awarded Writer of the Year by Be Inclusive Hospitality.

Acknowledgments

I'm really grateful to the many publicans who took time out of their busy day to speak to me – they work long hours in their kitchens and bars. I was given access to the pubs in Smethwick and West Bromwich through the trust of Bera Mahli at the Red Cow and Jinder Birring and Ray at the Prince of Wales. While my friends Meg and Gaurav Khanna at the Gladstone in South London offered constant support and reassurance that this project was worthwhile whenever I found it daunting.

The people who accompanied me on a lot of these travels, particularly Ishaan Puri, founder of White Rhino Brewing Company, and journalist Mark Machado, need to be thanked for keeping the grill experience communal. As do Nick Lichtenberg and Holly Regan for giving me their opinions on what a curious American traveller would think of British desi culture. Amir Deghan helped me on my journey – especially with photography and post-production tips – despite having some personal issues to deal with. And Neel Joshi was a great encyclopaedia to tap into, offering his guidance to the many Gujarati intuitions in London and beyond.

Desi pubs in general suffered from a lack of media coverage before bold commissions on the subject by *Pellicle*, *Good Beer Hunting* and *Atlas Obscura*. I would, therefore, like to thank Matthew Curtis, Claire Bullen and Alex Mayyasi for believing in the importance of this sidelined part of South Asian culture. I would also like to pay tribute to Alan Murphy, Commissioning Editor at CAMRA Books, for fighting for this project at the start and then driving me around a snowy Bradford towards its conclusion.

Thanks to the people who helped with the childcare of my two-year-old son and my six-year-old daughter while I was away – especially our amazing and endlessly flexible childminder, Sharon Clayson. But most of all I am forever grateful to my partner Clare Butterworth who tolerated endless trips which disrupted our daily life. Love you.

10 great reasons to join CAMRA

1	**CAMPAIGN** for great beer, cider and perry	**2**	Become a **BEER EXPERT**
3	Enjoy CAMRA **BEER FESTIVALS** in front of or behind the bar	**4**	**GET INVOLVED** and make new friends
5	Save **YOUR LOCAL**	**6**	Find the **BEST PUBS** **IN BRITAIN**
7	Get great **VALUE FOR** **MONEY**	**8**	**DISCOVER** pub heritage and the great outdoors
9	Enjoy great **HEALTH BENEFITS** (really!)	**10**	**HAVE YOUR SAY**

What's yours?

Discover your reason
and join the campaign today:

www.camra.org.uk/10reasons

Campaign
for
Real Ale